DEFINITIONS OF ABNORMALITY

Specification: Definitions of abnormality, including deviation from social norms, failure to function adequately, statistical infrequency and deviation from ideal mental health.

WHAT YOU NEED TO KNOW

- Outline and evaluate the following definitions of abnormality:
  - o Deviation from social norms
  - o Failure to function adequately
  - o Statistical infrequency
  - o Deviation from ideal mental health

Introduction

Psychopathology is the study of psychological disorders. One issue with studying mental health problems is how to identify when someone is psychologically unwell. Another cause for concern is how to determine if their behaviour differs from what is considered 'normal' and at what point should that person be classified as 'abnormal'? Consequently, psychologists and health professionals have put forward different **definitions of abnormality** in an attempt to understand abnormal behaviour. There are four key definitions: deviation from social norms; failure to function adequately; statistical infrequency; and deviation from ideal mental health.

Exam Hint: For each of these four key terms you are required to outline the definition, provide an example of how this could be seen in a person and evaluate the effectiveness of this as a definition of abnormality.

Deviation from Social Norms

A social norm is an unwritten rule about what is acceptable within a particular society. Therefore, according to this definition, a person is seen as abnormal if their thinking or behaviour violates these unwritten rules (social norms) about what is acceptable. For example, if you were to see someone walking around the streets of London practically naked, you would probably think they were abnormal. However, this same behaviour in a remote African tribe would be considered perfectly normal as part of their culture.

Evaluation of Deviation from Social Norms

- One issue with the **deviation from social norms** definition of abnormality is the idea of **cultural relativism**. Social norms differ between cultures and what is considered normal in one culture may be abnormal in another. For example, in approximately 75 countries in the world homosexuality is still illegal, and therefore considered abnormal. However, in the rest of the world homosexuality is considered normal. The result of this is that there is no global standard for defining behaviour as abnormal and therefore abnormality is not standardised.

- Furthermore, social norms change over time which raises an issue known as **hindsight bias.** For example, homosexuality was regarded as a mental illness in the UK until 1973, often resulting in institutionalisation, but is now simply considered a variation of normal behaviour. This means that, historically, reliance on the deviation from social norm definition of abnormality may have resulted in violations of human rights where people, by today's standards, are deemed 'abnormal'. It could be argued that diagnoses upon these grounds may have been given as a form of social control over minority groups as a means to exclude those who do not conform from society (Szas, 1974).

- How far an individual deviates from a social norm is mediated by the degree of severity and the context. For example, when someone breaks a social norm once this may not be deviant behaviour, but the persistent repetition of such behaviour could be evidence of psychological disturbance. Likewise, someone walking topless on a beach would be considered normal but, on the other hand, adopting the same attire for the office would be viewed as abnormal and possibly an indication of an underlying mental health problem. As a consequence, this definition fails to offer a complete explanation in its own right since it is related to degree and context.

Failure to Function Adequately

According to the **Failure to Function Adequately** (FFA) definition, a person is considered abnormal if they are unable to cope with the demands of everyday life and live independently in society. Furthermore, to be classified as abnormal, a person's behaviour should cause personal suffering and distress because of their failure to cope. However, they may also cause distress or discomfort to other people who observe their behaviour.

For example, someone who is suffering from depression may struggle to get out of bed in the morning and go to work, or they may find it difficult to communicate with their family and friends. Consequently, they would be considered abnormal as their depression is causing an inability to cope with the demands of everyday life (going to work), while their behaviour is also causing distress and discomfort to family members and friends.

Evaluation of Failure to Function Adequately

- One weakness of the failure to function adequately definition stems from **individual differences**. For example, one person with Obsessive Compulsive Disorder (OCD) may exhibit excessive rituals that prevent them from functioning adequately, as they constantly miss work; whereas, another person may suffer from the same excessive rituals, but find time to complete their rituals and always attend work on time. Therefore, despite the same psychological and behavioural symptoms, each person would be diagnosed differently according to this definition, thus questioning the validity of this definition.

- One strength of the failure to function adequately definition is that is considers the subjective **personal experiences** of the patient. This definition considers the thoughts and feelings of the person experiencing the issue and does not simply make a judgement without taking the personal viewpoint of the sufferer into consideration. This suggests that the failure to function definition is a useful model for assessing psychopathological behaviour.

- There is often confusion with distinguishing between failure to function adequately and deviation from social norms. On occasion, a behaviour which appears to be a failure to function adequately, such as not being able to go to work, may in fact also be a deviation from the social norm should that person be choosing to live an alternative lifestyle out of the common system for that society. It is therefore difficult to ascertain if this behaviour should be considered maladaptive. By labelling individuals who make such choices as 'failing', personal freedom is being quashed.

Statistical Infrequency

According to the Statistical Infrequency definition, a behaviour is seen as abnormal if it is statistically uncommon or not seen very often in society. Therefore, abnormality is determined by looking at the distribution of a particular behaviour within society.

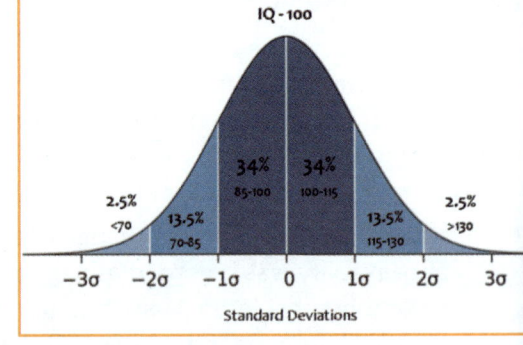

For example, the average IQ is approximately 100 and 65% of the population have an IQ in the region of 85 to 115. Furthermore, 95% of the population have an IQ in the region of 70 to 130. However, a small percentage of the population (approximately 5%) have an IQ below 70 or above 130 and these people are statistically uncommon and consequently, they would be classified as abnormal, according to this definition.

A normal distribution curve can be used to represent the proportions of the population who share a particular characteristic. The diagram (see left) demonstrates the distribution curve for IQ. At the extreme ends of the curve, 2.5% of the population has an IQ below 70, and 2.5% of the population has an IQ above 130. These people are statistically infrequent and therefore classed as being abnormal.

Evaluation of Statistical Infrequency

- One problem with the statistical infrequency definition of abnormality is the issue of **misdiagnosis**. Certain behaviours are statistically common; for example, approximately 10% of the population will experience depression at some point making this behaviour 'normal', technically. On the other hand, certain behaviours – for example, high IQ – are statistically uncommon and therefore considered abnormal despite their desirable nature. This is therefore a serious drawback of adopting the statistical infrequency definition in explaining abnormality and perhaps should not be used in isolation when making a diagnosis.

- A further issue with the statistical infrequency definition of abnormality is that **labelling** an individual as abnormal can be unhelpful. This is especially true, for example, of someone with a low IQ since they will be able to live quite happily without distress to themselves or others. Such a label may contribute to a poor self-image or become an invitation for discrimination. This means that being labelled as statistically infrequent could cause the person more distress than the condition itself.

- Some statistically infrequent behaviours labelled as abnormal could, in fact, be desirable traits. For example, having a very high IQ is very unusual, yet this characteristic could be hugely celebrated. Conversely, depression is known to be experienced by many people at some point in their lives and as such is considered common, but not desirable. Statistical infrequency as a definition of abnormality therefore needs to identify those behaviours which are both infrequent and undesirable to avoid this pitfall.

Deviation from Ideal Mental Health

Jahoda (1958) took a different approach to defining abnormality, suggesting that abnormal behaviour should be defined by the absence of particular (ideal) characteristics – in other words, behaviours which move away (deviate) from ideal mental health. This is similar to the approach taken by the medical profession for measures of physical health such as having blood pressure within the normal range, standard body temperature and so on. She proposed six principles of ideal mental health:

- Having a positive view of yourself (high self-esteem) with a strong sense of identity
- Being capable of personal growth and self-actualisation
- Being independent of others (autonomous) and self-regulating
- Having an accurate view of reality
- Being able to integrate and resist stress
- Being able to master your environment (love, friendships, work, and leisure time)

Therefore, if an individual does not demonstrate one of these criteria, they would be classified as abnormal according to this definition. For example, someone suffering from depression may have a negative view of themselves and would therefore be classified as abnormal.

Evaluation of Deviation from Ideal Mental Health

- One weakness of the deviation from ideal mental health definition is the **unrealistic criteria** proposed by Jahoda. There are times when everyone will experience stress and negativity, for example, when grieving following the death of a loved one. However, according to this definition, these people would be classified as abnormal, irrespective of the circumstances which are outside their control. With the high standards set by these criteria, how many need to be absent for diagnosis to occur must also be questioned.

- However, one strength of Jahoda's definition is that it takes a **positive** and **holistic** stance. Firstly, the definition focuses on positive and desirable behaviours, rather than considering just negative and undesirable behaviours. Secondly, the definition considers the whole person, taking into account a multitude of factors that can affect their health and well-being. Therefore, a strength of the deviation from ideal mental health definition of abnormality is that it is comprehensive, covering a broad range of criteria.

- An issue with Jahoda's definition of abnormality is **cultural relativism**. Some of the criteria for ideal mental health could be considered Western in origin. For example, her emphasis on personal growth and development may be considered overly self-centred in other countries of the world who favour community over individualism. Likewise, independence within collectivist cultures is not fostered thus making the definition **culture bound**.

Exam Hint: Students can often muddle up the four definitions, so it is important to invest time revising the similarities and differences between them to avoid losing credit in the exam for descriptions which do not match the correct key term.

Extension Evaluation: Issues and Debates

- The development of criteria takes a **nomothetic** approach by identifying a list of factors through which to diagnose abnormal behaviour. Yet, everyone is an individual, so perhaps an **idiographic** approach to this area of psychology might be more fruitful.

- **Ethnocentricity** is another issue with defining abnormality, especially regarding Jahoda's criteria for ideal mental health. For example, 'being independent and self-regulating' applies particularly to individualistic societies wherein independence is valued as a quality and is not seen as selfishness, which might be the case in collectivist societies who favour working together more.

Possible Exam Questions

1. Which of the following is not one of the criteria for ideal mental health as suggested by Jahoda? (1 mark)
    a) Being autonomous and self-reliant
    b) Ability to adjust to new situations
    c) Following the rules of society
    d) Developing to your full capability

2. Hannah is in her second year at university but she finds that most days she does not have the motivation to attend lectures or even get out of bed to wash and dress. Using your knowledge and understanding of psychopathology, identify which definition of abnormality is most suitable for explaining Hannah's behaviour. (1 mark)

3. Briefly outline **one** definition of abnormality. (2 marks)

4. Explain what is meant by deviation from social norms. (2 marks)
Exam Hint: Use the number of marks available for a question as a guide on how much elaboration to provide in your answer.

5. Identify **two** of the following criteria which are examples from Jahoda's definition of ideal mental health (2 marks)
    a) A lack of inhibition
    b) Over dependence on other
    c) Maladaptiveness
    d) Resistant to stress
    e) Environmental mastery

6. Define what is meant by statistical infrequency in the context of defining abnormal behaviour. (2 marks)
Exam Hint: To achieve full credit on this question a clean and coherent definition must be provided, such as: statistical infrequency is when an individual's characteristics, thinking or overt behaviour is considered numerically rare and therefore is considered abnormal.

7. Rosalee has been told by her doctor that she has ideal mental health. An example to support this claim is that she can, for example, resist stress. Identify **two** other criteria for ideal mental health that you could expect Rosalee to demonstrate. (2 marks)
Exam Hint: Since resistance to stress has already been suggested, answers that refer to this again will not receive any credit.

8. Briefly explain **one** limitation of the failure to function adequately definition of abnormality. (2 marks)
Exam Hint: Sound answers to this question are most likely to consider context as an issue or cultural relativism.

9. Name two criteria for ideal mental health as suggested by Jahoda. (2 marks)

10. Apart from deviation from ideal mental health, outline one definition of abnormality. (3 marks)
Exam Hint: While students are often able to define these key terms accurately, many students fail to pick up further marks because they struggle with elaboration. An easy way to ensure that students pick up all available marks is to provide an example related to the definition. For example: One other definition of abnormality is referred to as deviation from social norms. A social norm is an unwritten rule in a particular society, such as wearing shoes. Any behaviour which goes against basic expectations within that culture, e.g. walking barefoot, will be considered abnormal.

11. The four main definitions of abnormality are listed below (**1–4**).
    1 Statistical infrequency
    2 Deviation from ideal mental health
    3 Failure to function adequately
    4 Deviation from social norms

Read the descriptions of abnormal behaviour in the table below. Choose the most appropriate definition to match each description. Fill in the table by writing either **1** or **2** or **3** or **4** in the box at the end of the statement. Use any letter only **once**. (3 marks)

Behaviour which indicated incapacity to manage everyday life	
Behaviour which is uncommon and not shown by many individuals	
Behaviour which does not fit the conventions of what would be expected	

11. Evaluate deviation from ideal mental health as a definition of abnormality. (4 marks)

Exam hint: Although cultural relativism is a valid limitation, many students struggle to use this key term effectively. In this instance, a more comprehensive answer would focus on how Jahoda's criteria, specifically personal growth and development, were very Western and some cultures do not value autonomy. For example, collectivist cultures favour working together to meet a common goal rather an individual succeeding alone at the expense of the group which means that this is not a universal definition of abnormality.

12. One definition of abnormality is failure to function adequately. Identify and explain two other definitions. (6 marks)

Exam Hint: Remember there are two command words within this question so definitions must be explained rather than simply stated / identified for full credit to be awarded.

13. Outline **two** definitions of abnormality. (6 marks)

Exam Hint: Students need to make sure that any examples that they use to enhance their answer are indeed related to psychopathology or they will not receive any credit.

14. Abnormality can be defined as having an uncommon behaviour trait. Discuss the statistical infrequency definition of abnormality. (6 marks)

Exam Hint: The examiner is looking for a clear and accurate explanation of the term 'statistical infrequency' as a definition of abnormality. Be sure to refer to the fact that statistical infrequency means that an individual's thinking or behaviour would be considered an indication of abnormality if it was seen to be numerically rare/uncommon/anomalous.

15. Read the following excerpt which appeared in a magazine article and then answer the question that follows.

    Has hoarding become a 'new' mental illness?
    Most people can throw away the things they don't need anymore. However, it has been revealed that 1 in 1000 people suffer from a hoarding disorder. This is characterised by extreme anxiety about parting with items which clutter the living or working environment.
    Aside from 'deviation from ideal mental health', outline **three** other definitions of abnormality. Refer to the scenario above in your response. (6 marks)

16. Keith is a 50-year-old office manager who often has a temper tantrum when things do not go his way at work. When he goes to speak to his colleagues at their desk, he often invades their personal space by standing too close to them, which makes them feel awkward. When one of his team informed him their brother had died, he laughed out loud.

    Identify **one** definition of abnormality that could be applied to define Keith's behaviour, justifying your selection. Explain **one** limitation of abnormal behaviour in this way. (6 marks)

Exam Hint: This question requires students to utilise their application skills to demonstrate thorough knowledge and understanding of definitions of abnormality while engaging with the scenario. Most candidates will probably choose deviation from social norms but can equally choose either failure to function adequately or deviation from ideal mental health, as long as it is applied successfully to Keith's behaviour.

17. Whether someone should be defined as abnormal or not can be a very difficult decision to make. This is often because it can be hard to decide where behaviour falls on the continuum from normal to abnormal.

    Discuss **two or more** definitions of abnormality. (12/16 marks)

Exam Hint: In essay questions such as this it is important to strike a balance between AO1 and AO3 marks available to ensure that the top mark band can be accessed without restriction.

18. Outline and evaluate **one or more** definition of abnormality, other than deviation from social norms. (12/16 marks)

Exam Hint: This question asks students to refer to definition/s other than deviation from social norms and those students who do not read the question carefully will fail to achieve full credit.

CLINICAL CHARACTERISTICS

Specification: The behavioural, emotional and cognitive characteristics of phobias, depression and obsessive compulsive disorder (OCD).

WHAT YOU NEED TO KNOW

▪ Outline the behavioural, emotional and cognitive characteristics of:
     o Phobias
     o Depression
     o Obsessive Compulsive Disorder (OCD)

Introduction

In the UK, psychiatrists use the ICD (International Statistical Classification of Diseases and Related Health Problems) diagnostic system to diagnose psychological disorders. Three psychological disorders include: phobias, depression and obsessive compulsive disorder (OCD). The ICD outlines possible symptoms in relation to phobias, depression and OCD and these symptoms can be categorised as behavioural, emotional and cognitive.

Phobias

Phobias are categorised as an anxiety disorder which cause an irrational fear of a particular object or situation. There are three categories of phobia:

- **Simple (specific) phobias**
- **Social phobias**
- **Agoraphobia**

Simple Phobias

Simple, or specific, phobias are the most common type of phobia. This is where a person fears a specific object in the environment, for example arachnophobia, the fear of spiders. **Simple phobias** are further divided into four categories: **animal phobias, injury phobias, situational phobias and natural phobias.** Common animal phobias include arachnophobia (see above) and ophidiophobia; the fear of snakes. Injury phobias include haematophobia, the fear of blood. Situational phobias include aerophobia, the fear of flying and natural phobias include hydrophobia, the fear of water.

Social Phobias

Social phobias involve feelings of anxiety in social situations, for example, when giving a speech in public. Sufferers feel like they are being judged, which leads to feelings of inadequacy and apprehension. Social phobias are further divided into three categories: **performance phobias**, **interaction phobias** and **generalised phobias**.

Performance phobias result in feelings of anxiety when performing in public, for example, eating in a restaurant with friends; interaction phobias result in feelings of anxiety when mixing with others, for example, when answering questions during an interview and generalised phobias result in feelings of anxiety when other people are present, for example, when in a large crowd at a music concert.

Agoraphobia

Agoraphobia is a fear of open or public spaces and sufferers may experience panic attacks and anxiety, which make them feel vulnerable in open spaces.

Agoraphobia can be caused by simple phobias and/or social phobias. For example, the simple phobia mysophobia, which is the fear of contamination, could lead to a fear of public spaces.

Behavioural Characteristics: The behavioural characteristics of phobias can be divided into two characteristics: **avoidance** and **panic.**

The key behavioural characteristic of a phobia is avoidance. If a person with a phobia is presented with the object or situation they fear, their immediate response is to avoid it. For example, a person with arachnophobia will avoid being near spiders and people with a social phobia will avoid being in large crowds. However, people are not always able to avoid their fears and sometimes they come face-to-face with an object or situation they fear, which results in panic, causing high levels of stress and anxiety. Sometimes, the fear response is so intense, it results in a person 'freezing', which is part of the 'fight or flight' fear response. The freezing response is an adaptive response to make a predator think that their prey is dead.

Emotional Characteristics: The key emotional characteristics of a phobia, are **excessive** and **unreasonable fear**, **anxiety** and **panic**. An excessive emotional response is triggered by the presence, or the anticipation of, a specific object or situation.

Cognitive Characteristics: The cognitive characteristics of phobias are also divided into two characteristics: **selective attention** and **irrational beliefs**.

If a person with a phobia is presented with an object or situation they fear, they will find it difficult to direct their attention elsewhere. Therefore, a person's **selective attention** will cause them to become fixated on the object they fear, because of their irrational beliefs about the danger posed.

Furthermore, a person's phobia is defined by their **irrational thinking** towards the object or situation. For example, a person with arachnophobia may believe that all spiders are dangerous and deadly, despite the fact that no spiders in the UK are actually deadly.

Depression

Depression is a category of mood disorders, which is often divided into two main types: **unipolar** and **bipolar** disorder (formerly known as manic-depression).

To be given a diagnosis of depression, sufferers are required to display at least five symptoms, every day, for at least two weeks.

Behavioural Characteristics: There are numerous behavioural characteristics associated with depression, including: loss of energy, sleep disturbance and changes in appetite. Firstly, there is often a change in activity level; sufferers of depression often experience a **reduction in energy** and constantly feel tired. Furthermore, sufferers often experience disturbances with their **sleeping pattern**, with some sufferers sleeping significantly more, while others experience insomnia, which is an inability to sleep. Finally, sufferers often experience changes in **appetite**, which cause significant weight changes. Some sufferers will eat less and lose weight, while others will eat more and gain weight.

Emotional Characteristics: They key emotional characteristic of depression is a depressed mood, or feelings of sadness. Sufferers of depression will often experience the following: **depressed mood**, **feelings of worthlessness** and **lack of interest or pleasure** in all activities.

Although a depressed mood is the most common emotional characteristic of depression, some sufferers experience **anger**, which can be directed at themselves, or others. Anger can also lead to self-harming behaviours.

Cognitive Characteristics: In addition to the emotional and behavioural characteristics, sufferers of depression often have a **diminished ability to concentrate** and a tendency to **focus on the negative**.

Sufferers of depression find it difficult to pay or maintain attention and are often slower in responding to, or making, decisions. Furthermore, they are inclined to focus on the negative aspects of a situation, while ignoring the positives and in some cases, experience recurrent thoughts of self-harm, death or suicide.

Obsessive Compulsive Disorder

OCD (Obsessive Compulsive Disorder), like phobias, is classified as an anxiety disorder and has two main components, **obsessions** and **compulsions.** Obsessions are reoccurring and persistent thoughts and compulsions are repetitive behaviours. 70% of OCD sufferers experience combined obsessions and compulsions. However, 20% experience just obsessions and 10% experience just compulsions.

Behavioural Characteristics: The behavioural component of OCD centres on the compulsive behaviour, and for sufferers of OCD compulsions have two properties. Firstly, compulsions are **repetitive** in nature and sufferers will often feel compelled to repeat a behaviour such as repetitive hand washing. Secondly, compulsions are used to manage or **reduce anxiety.** For example, the excessive hand washing is caused by an excessive fear of germs and bacteria and is therefore a direct response to the obsession.

Emotional Characteristics: The emotional characteristics of OCD are mainly characterised by **anxiety** which is caused by the obsessions. However, some sufferers of OCD also experience **depression**. Obsessions are persistent and/or forbidden thoughts and ideas, which cause high levels of **anxiety** in OCD sufferers. Furthermore, OCD can often lead to **depression**, as the anxiety experienced can result in a low mood and loss of pleasure in everyday activities because these everyday tasks are being interrupted by obsessive thoughts and repetitive compulsions.

Cognitive Characteristics: Obsessive thoughts are the main cognitive feature of OCD. Examples of recurring thoughts include: fear of contamination, by dirt or germs; fear of safety, by leaving doors or windows open; religious fears of retribution for being immoral; perfectionism, a fear of not being the best. For sufferers of OCD, these thoughts occur over and over again.

Some sufferers of OCD adopt **cognitive strategies** to deal with their obsessions. For example, suffers with religious obsessions may pray over and over, to reduce their feelings of being immoral. Furthermore, sufferers of OCD know that their obsessions and compulsions are irrational and experience **selective attention** directed towards the anxiety-generating stimuli (similar to the selective attention found in phobias).

	BEHAVIOURAL	EMOTIONAL	COGNITIVE
PHOBIAS	Avoidance of the stimulus and panic when the feared object is encountered.	Excessive and unreasonable fear and anxiety.	Becoming fixated on the object of fear and irrational thinking towards the object or situation.
DEPRESSION	Reduction in energy and constantly feeling tired, disturbed sleep pattern and changes in appetite.	Depressed mood, feelings of worthlessness and lack of interest or pleasure in everyday activities.	Diminished ability to concentrate and a tendency to focus on the negative.
OCD	Repetitive compulsions used to manage or reduce anxiety.	Anxiety and depression caused by the interruption to daily life.	Obsessive thoughts and selective attention directed towards the anxiety-generating stimuli.

Extension Evaluation: Issues and Debates

- Because of a lack of cross-cultural statistics on these disorders, most of the research and information comes from organisations based in Western cultures, which inevitably leads to an **ethnocentric bias**.

- There is an aspect of **environmental determinism** in that phobias and OCD especially can be seen as learned responses to stress triggers. Phobias and OCD both allow for stress reduction, the first by avoidance and the second through obsessive rituals.

Possible Exam Questions

1. Define what is meant by the term 'phobia'. (2 marks)

2. Identify which **two** of the following statements are behavioural characteristics of depression. (2 marks)
    a. Lack of interest in everyday activities
    b. Sense of worthlessness
    c. Disrupted sleep patterns
    d. Change in appetite
    e. Poor concentration levels

3. What is the difference between an obsession and a compulsion? (2 marks)
Exam Hint: If students are asked in the exam to compare two concepts, such as an obsession and a compulsion, conjunctions such as 'however', 'alternatively', 'in contrast' or 'on the other hand' should be used to illustrate a clear comparison between the two key term definitions.

4. Explain the difference between behavioural, emotional and cognitive characteristics. (2 marks)

5. Deborah has been feeling unwell recently and has gone to see her doctor to report her most persistent symptoms. Emotionally, she is feeling empty and that she has a lack of control over her anger which she is directing towards her husband. Lately, she has noticed that she has much less energy to do the usual day-to-day activities and she has even stopped enjoying her favourite pastime of gardening. She has started to think that things will never change and that she will always feel like this.
Identify what mental disorder is the doctor most likely to diagnose Deborah as suffering from and justify your choice. (3 marks)

6. Briefly outline the behavioural characteristics of obsessive compulsive disorder (OCD). (3 marks)
Exam Hint: In order to tackle this question well, students need to make appropriate reference to both compulsions and avoidance behaviour.

7. Outline the cognitive characteristics of either depression **or** phobias. (3 marks)
Exam Hint: Be sure to read the question carefully and only chose to outline the cognitive characteristics of one disorder, not both.

8. Outline the characteristics of depression. You may refer to behavioural, emotional and/or cognitive characteristics in your answer. (4 marks).
Exam Hint: This question required students to outline the different characteristic of depression. There is a risk that some students may present a wealth of material, often far exceeding the four marks available. Most students will be best focusing on two of the three types of characteristics.

9. Outline the characteristics of obsessive compulsive disorder (OCD). (4 marks)
Exam Hint: Better answers relating to OCD will always refer to both obsession and compulsions with qualifying statements about the frequency of these.

10. Outline the behavioural, emotional and cognitive characteristics of any **one** of the following mental health disorders: depression, phobias, obsessive compulsive disorders. (6 marks)

PHOBIAS

Specification: The behavioural approach to explaining and treating phobias: the two-process model, including classical and operant conditioning; systematic desensitisation, including relaxation and use of hierarchy; flooding.

WHAT YOU NEED TO KNOW

▪ Outline and evaluate the behavioural approach to explaining phobias, through the two-process model:
   ○ The acquisition of phobias through classical conditioning
   ○ The maintenance of phobias through operant conditioning
 ▪ Outline and evaluate behavioural treatments of phobias, including:
   ○ Systematic desensitisation
   ○ Flooding

Introduction

According to the behavioural approach, abnormal behaviour can be caused by: 1) classical conditioning, 2) operant conditioning and 3) social learning theory. Mowrer (1947) proposed a two-process model, to explain how phobias are learned through classical conditioning and maintained through operant conditioning.

Explaining Phobias – The Two-Process Model

According to the two-process model, phobias can be acquired through classical conditioning and associative learning.

Classical Conditioning

Classical conditioning is a process of learning by associating two stimuli together to condition (learn) a response. According to the theory of classical conditioning, phobias can be acquired through associative learning. The process of classical conditioning can explain how we learn to associate something we do not fear (neutral stimulus), for example a lift, with something which triggers a fear response (unconditioned stimulus), for example being trapped. After an association has formed, the lift (now a conditioned stimulus) causes a response of fear (conditioned response) and consequently, we develop a phobia of lift, following a single incident of being trapped in a lift.

Key Study: Watson & Rayner (1920)

Aim: To investigate whether a fear response could be learned through classical conditioning in humans.

Method: Their participant was an 11-month-old child called 'Little Albert'. Before the experiment, Watson & Rayner noted that Albert showed no response to various objects, in particular, a white rat. In order to examine if they could induce a fear response, Watson & Rayner struck a metal bar with a hammer behind Little Albert's head, causing a very loud noise which startled him, every time he went to reach for the rat. They did this three times.

Results: Thereafter, whenever they showed Little Albert the white rat, he began to cry.

Conclusion: This experiment demonstrated that a fear response could be induced through the process of classical conditioning in humans. In addition, Little Albert also developed a fear towards similar objects, including a white Santa Claus beard. The experiment revealed that Little Albert had generalised his fear to other white furry objects.

Operant Conditioning

Although classical conditioning can explain why we develop a phobia, it struggles to explain why our phobias do not decay over time. For example, it is unlikely that a person will get trapped in every lift they use and therefore it would be reasonable to assume that a person's phobia of lifts should weaken every time they travel in a lift and don't get trapped. However, most phobias are long-term and according to Mowrer, our phobias are maintained through operant conditioning.

According to the theory of operant conditioning, phobias can be negatively reinforced. This is where a behaviour is strengthened because an unpleasant consequence is removed. For example, if a person with a phobia of lifts always takes the stairs, then they are constantly avoiding their phobia. This avoidance reduces the person's feelings of anxiety and so negatively reinforces their behaviour, making the person more likely to repeat this behaviour (avoidance) in the future. As a result, a person will continue to avoid lifts and maintain their phobia.

Therefore, according to the two-process model, phobias are initiated through classical conditioning (learning through association) and maintained through operant conditioning (negative reinforcement).

Evaluation of the Behavioural Approach to Explaining Phobias

- **Research evidence** supports the behavioural explanation of phobias. Watson & Rayner (1920) demonstrated the process of classical conditioning in the formation of a phobia in Little Albert, who was conditioned to fear white rats. This supports the idea that classical conditioning is involved in acquiring phobias in humans and that generalisation can occur to other phobic stimuli. However, since this was a case study, it is difficult to generalise the findings to other children or even adults due to the unique nature of the investigation.

- Another strength of the behavioural explanation is its **application** to therapy. The behaviourist ideas have been used to develop treatments, including systematic desensitisation and flooding. Systematic desensitisation helps people to unlearn their fears, using the principles of classical conditioning, while flooding prevents people from avoiding their phobias and stops the negative reinforcement from taking place. Consequently, these therapies have been successfully used to treat people with phobias, providing further support for the effectiveness of the behaviourist explanation.

- The behavioural explanation for the development of phobias ignores the role of cognition (thinking): phobias may develop as a result of irrational thinking, not just learning. For example, sufferers of claustrophobia (a fear of confined spaces) may think: 'I am going to be trapped in this lift and suffocate', which is an irrational thought that is not taken into consideration in the behaviourist explanation. Furthermore, the cognitive approach has also led to the development of **cognitive behavioural therapy (CBT)**, a treatment which is said to be more successful than the behaviourist treatments.

- There is a claim that the behavioural approach may not provide a complete explanation of phobias. For example, **Bounton (2007)** highlights the fact that evolutionary factors could play a role in phobias, especially if the avoidance of a particular stimulus (e.g. snakes) could have caused pain or even death to our ancestors. Consequently, evolutionary psychologists suggest that some phobias (e.g. snakes and heights) are not learned but are in fact innate, as such phobias acted as a survival mechanism for our ancestors. This innate predisposition to certain phobias is called **biological preparedness** (Seligman, 1971) and casts doubt on the two-process model since it suggests that there is more to phobias than learning.

Treating Phobias

There are two behavioural treatments for phobias: systematic desensitisation and flooding. Both therapies use the principles of classical conditioning to replace a person's phobia with a new response – relaxation.

Systematic Desensitisation

Systematic desensitisation uses **counter-conditioning** to unlearn the maladaptive response to a situation or object, by eliciting another response (relaxation). There are three critical components to systematic desensitisation:
1) Fear hierarchy
2) Relaxation training
3) Reciprocal inhibition

Firstly, the client and therapist work together to develop a fear hierarchy, where they rank the phobic situation from least to most terrifying. For example:

ACTIVITY	FEAR LEVEL (0-100)
Stroking a dog	90
Going to a park with a dog walker	80
Watching a real-life dog show	50
Watching a cartoon dog show	40
Looking at a picture of a dog	30

Thereafter, an individual is taught relaxation techniques, such as breathing techniques, progressive muscle relaxation strategies, or mental imagery techniques.

The final component of systematic desensitisation involves exposing the patient to their phobic situation, while relaxed. According to systematic desensitisation, two emotional states cannot exist at the same time; a theory known as **reciprocal inhibition**. Therefore, a person is unable to be anxious and relaxed at the same time and the relaxation should overtake the fear. The patient starts at the bottom of the fear hierarchy and when the patient can remain relaxed in the presence of the least feared stimulus, they gradually progress to the next level. The patient gradually moves their way up the hierarchy until they are completely relaxed in the most feared situation; at this point systematic desensitisation is successful and a new response to the stimulus has been learned, replacing the phobia.

Evaluation of Systematic Desensitisation

- One strength of systematic desensitisation comes from research evidence that demonstrates the effectiveness of this treatment for phobias. **McGrath *et al.* (1990)** found that 75% of patients with phobias were successfully treated using systematic desensitisation. This was particularly true when using in vivo techniques in which the patient came into direct contact with the feared stimulus rather than simply imagining (in vitro). This shows that systematic desensitisation is effective when treating specific phobias, especially when using in vivo techniques.

- Further support comes from **Gilroy *et al.* (2002)** who examined 42 patients with arachnophobia (fear of spiders). Each patient was treated using three 45-minute systematic desensitisation sessions. When examined three months and 33 months later, the systematic desensitisation group were less fearful than a control group (who were only taught relaxation techniques). This provides further support for systematic desensitisation as an effective treatment for phobias in the long-term.

- However, systematic desensitisation is not effective in treating all phobias. Patients with phobias which have not developed through a personal experience (classical conditioning), such as a fear of snakes, are not effectively treated using systematic desensitisation. Some psychologists believe that certain phobias have an evolutionary survival benefit and are not the result of learning. This highlights a limitation of systematic desensitisation, which is ineffective in treating **evolutionary** phobias which have an **innate** basis.

- Systematic desensitisation is often favoured as a treatment for phobias in comparison to flooding, as it is more **ethical** in nature. In comparison to flooding treatment for phobias many patients report a preference for systematic desensitisation as it does not cause the same levels of distress that can occur when presented with the fear-inducing stimulus immediately. This is reflected in the high number of patients who persist with systematic desensitisation providing low attrition rates. It is therefore considered a more appropriate treatment for individuals who may have learning difficulties or suffer from severe anxiety disorders since learning the relaxation techniques can be a positive and pleasant experience.

Flooding

Flooding is a behavioural therapy which, rather than exposing a person to their phobic stimulus gradually, exposes the individual to the anxiety-inducing stimulus immediately. For example, a person with a phobia of dogs would be placed in a room with a dog and asked to stroke the dog straight away. This intense exposure is done over an extended period of time in a safe and controlled manner.

With flooding, a person is unable to avoid (negatively reinforce) their phobia and through continuous exposure, anxiety levels eventually decrease. Since the option of employing avoidant behaviour is removed, **extinction** will soon occur since fear is a time-limited response to a situation which eventually subsides. As exhaustion sets in for the individual they may begin to feel a sense of calm and relief which creates a new positive association to the stimulus.

Evaluation of Flooding

- One strength of flooding is it provides a **cost-effective** treatment for phobias. Research has suggested that flooding is equally effective to other treatments, including systematic desensitisation and cognition therapies (**Ougrin, 2011**), but takes much less time in achieving these positive results. This is a strength of the treatment because patients cure their phobias more quickly and it is therefore more cost-effective for health service providers who do not have to fund longer options.

- Although flooding is considered a cost-effective solution, it can be **highly traumatic** for patients since it purposefully elicits a high level of anxiety. **Wolpe (1969)** recalled a case with a patient becoming so intensely anxious that she required hospitalisation. Although it is not unethical as patients provide fully informed consent, many do not complete their treatment because the experience is too stressful. Therefore, initiating flooding treatment is sometimes a waste of time and money if patients do not engage in or complete the full course of their treatment.

- Even though flooding is highly effective for simple (specific) phobias, the treatment is less effective for other types of phobia, including social phobia and agoraphobia. Some psychologists suggest that social phobias are caused by irrational thinking and are not caused by an unpleasant experience (or learning through classical conditioning). Therefore, more complex phobias cannot be treated by behavioural treatments and may be more responsive to other forms of treatment, for example, cognitive behavioural therapy (CBT), which treats the irrational thinking.

- An issue for behavioural therapies such as flooding and systematic desensitisation is **symptom substitution**. This means that although one phobia may be successfully removed through counter-conditioning another may appear in its place. If symptoms are treated and removed, the underlying cause may remain and simply resurface under a new guise. Research in this area is mixed, however, and heavily disputed by behaviourists.

Extension Evaluation: Issues and Debates

- The behavioural explanation for the development of phobias has been criticised for being **reductionist** and overly simplistic in its reduction of human behaviour to a simple stimulus-response association. It ignores the role of cognition (thinking) in the formation of phobias, and cognitive psychologists suggest that phobias may develop as a result of irrational thinking, not just learning. Therefore, it is also subject to **environmental determinism** in ignoring the role of individual **free will** in the formation of phobias. Not every person bitten by a dog develops a phobia of dogs, for example, so other processes must be at play.

- The behavioural approach is a **nomothetic** approach that has created universal laws regarding the formation and maintenance of phobias. Yet, if we accept individual cognition plays a part, a more **idiographic** approach may be effective.

Possible Exam Questions

1. Which of the following principles does not underpin systematic desensitisation? (1 mark)
    a. Counter-conditioning, b. Reciprocal inhibition, c. Classical conditioning, d. Counter-balancing

2. Explain **one** limitation of flooding as a treatment for phobias. (2 marks)

3. Explain **one** limitation of systematic desensitisation. (2 marks)
Exam Hint: Note that systematic desensitisation is considered one of the most ethical behavioural therapies because clients are also taught relaxation techniques so ethical issues will not be credited as a valid limitation.

4. Suggest **one** advantage of using flooding over systematic desensitisation as a treatment for a phobia of spiders. (2 marks)

5. Explain why using systematic desensitisation might be more appropriate than using flooding as a behavioural treatment for phobias. (2 marks)
Exam Hint: The advice to students for this type of question is to simply answer the question. Often answers start with "Using systematic desensitisation might be more appropriate than using flooding as a behavioural treatment for phobias", and such answers face the risk of running out of space before they have actually started to provide accurate and detailed answers.

6. Outline what is involved in systematic desensitisation as a treatment for phobias. (3 marks)
Exam Hint: In order to demonstrate sound understanding, include reference to the anxiety/fear hierarchy, relaxation techniques and the gradual working up through the hierarchy.

7. Describe what flooding involves as a behavioural treatment for phobias. (3 marks)

8. Tom has a fear of dogs. His fear stops him going to his local park for walks in case he sees a dog there. Explain how systematic desensitisation could be used as a treatment for Tom's phobia. (4 marks)
Exam Hint: The main challenge for students here is to ensure sufficient engagement with the scenario. Simply mentioning Tom's name is not evidence enough of engaging with the scenario. Students need to provide some specific examples of the different stages on a hierarchy intended to overcome the phobia of encountering a dog in public to gain full marks.

9. Adam is in his mid-thirties and has had a phobia of clowns since one jumped up on him at a friends' birthday party when he was a little boy. Red noses and face painting still cause Adam extreme anxiety today. He therefore avoids situations such as birthday parties, fancy dress events and theme parks if there might be clowns present.

    Explain how the behavioural approach might be used to explain Adam's phobia of clowns. (4 marks)

10. Briefly describe the behavioural approach to explaining phobias and discuss **one** limitation of this. (6 marks)

Exam hint: Ensure that your description is always clearly linked to phobias, for example, through an illustration. Better answers will typically elaborate on both elements of the two-process model of phobias. Students can often find the three-mark format challenging when applied to the explanation of a single limitation (or strength) so be sure to state your point, provide evidence for that argument and then explain using key terminology, where appropriate.

11. Psychologists who subscribe to the behavioural approach of explaining human behaviour believe that all behaviour – normal and abnormal – is learned. Outline and evaluate how the behavioural approach explains phobias. (12/16 marks)

Exam Hint: Answers will remain in the lower mark band if students fail to make the link between the learning processes and how they apply to abnormality – in this case, phobias. Evaluative commentary can consider the successful therapies that this approach has developed, although detailed description of flooding or systematic desensitisation is not creditworthy material for the outline element of this question.

12. Discuss the behavioural approach to treating phobias. (12/16 marks)

Exam Hint: To gain all of the AO1 marks that are available for this type of question students must avoid 'sketchy' descriptions of key concepts, such as 'anxiety hierarchy', by fully elaborating on what this involves. When assembling an evaluative argument centred around 'cost', 'time' or similar, ensure the reasoning is based on comparison to a treatment that would be cheaper or faster.

13. Sebastian has a severe phobia of birds. His phobia began when he was four years old. A pigeon scared him when it flew down and stole his ice cream! He is now ten years old and so scared that he will not play in the playground at break for fear of seeing a bird.

    Outline and evaluate systematic desensitisation as a treatment for phobias and refer to Sebastian in your answer. (16 marks)

Exam Hint: Students need to ensure that they provide elaborate descriptions of key concepts (e.g. fear/anxiety hierarchy) to achieve a top mark band. Furthermore, many students make evaluative comments based on 'time', 'cost' or 'effort' involved but rarely develop these points enough to achieve top marks. When using these evaluative points, students need to develop their points fully or make a comparison with another treatment apparent.

DEPRESSION

Specification: The cognitive approach to explaining and treating depression: Beck's negative triad and Ellis's ABC model; cognitive behaviour therapy (CBT), including challenging irrational thoughts.

WHAT YOU NEED TO KNOW

▪ Outline and evaluate the cognitive approach to explaining depression, including:
     o Becks Cognitive Triad
     o Ellis's ABC Model
 ▪ Outline and evaluate cognitive treatments of depression, including:
     o Cognitive Behavioural Therapy (CBT)
     o Challenging of irrational thoughts

Introduction
According to the cognitive approach, emotional problems are the result of **cognitive distortions** (irrational thinking) and there are two key cognitive theories, which attempt to explain depression:
▪ **Beck's Cognitive Triad**
▪ **Ellis's Irrational Thinking (ABC Model)**

Explaining Depression: Beck's Cognitive Triad (1963)
Beck claimed that depression is caused by negative self-schemas maintaining the **cognitive triad:** a negative and irrational view of ourselves, our future and the world around us. For sufferers of

NEGATIVE VIEWS ABOUT THE WORLD
"everyone is against me because I'm worthless"

NEGATIVE VIEWS ABOUT THE FUTURE
"I'll NEVER be good"

NEGATIVE VIEWS ABOUT ONESELF
"I'm worthless"

depression, these thoughts occur automatically and are symptomatic of depressed people.

Negative self-schemas: A schema is a 'package' of knowledge, which stores information and ideas about our self and the world around us. These schemas are developed during childhood and according to Beck, depressed people possess negative self-schemas, which may come from negative experiences, for example, criticism from parents, peers or even teachers. Examples of **negative self-schemas** are: an **ineptness schema**, which makes sufferers expect to fail; a **self-blame schema** that makes them feel responsible for any misfortunes; a negative **self-evaluation schema** that constantly reminds them of their worthlessness.

Cognitive biases: Beck found that depressed people are more likely to focus on the negative aspects of a situation, while ignoring the positives. These distort information, a process known as **cognitive bias**. Beck detailed numerous cognitive biases, two of which are: **overgeneralisations** and **catastrophising**. For example, a depressed person may make **overgeneralisations**, where they make a sweeping conclusion based on a single incident, for example: *'I've failed one end-of-unit test and therefore I'm going to fail ALL of my AS exams!'* Alternatively, a depressed person may experience **catastrophising**, where they exaggerate a minor setback and believe that it's a complete disaster, for example: *'I've failed one end-of-unit test and therefore I am never going to study at university or get a good job!'*

According to Beck, negative self-schemas and cognitive biases maintain the negative triad which is a negative view of three key aspects of a person's life which lead to depression. These include:
- The self – 'Nobody loves me.'
- The world – 'The world is an unfair place.'
- The future – 'I will always be a failure.'

Explaining Depression: Ellis's ABC Model

Ellis took a different approach to explaining depression and started by explaining what is required for 'good' mental health. According to Ellis, good mental health is the result of rational thinking which allows people to be happy and pain free, whereas depression is the result of irrational thinking, which prevents us from being happy and pain free.

Ellis's ABC model proposed a three-stage model to explain how irrational thoughts could lead to depression.

A	**ACTIVATING EVENT**	An event occurs, for example, you pass a friend in the corridor at school and he/she ignores you, despite the fact you said 'hello'.
B	**BELIEFS**	Your belief is your interpretation of the event, which could either be **rational** or **irrational**: • A **rational** interpretation of the event might be that your friend is very busy and possibly stressed, and he/she simply didn't see or hear you. • An **irrational** interpretation of the event might be that your friend dislikes you and never wants to talk to you again.
C	**CONSEQUENCES**	According to Ellis, rational beliefs lead to healthy emotional outcomes (for example, *'I will talk to my friend later and see if he/she is okay'*), whereas irrational beliefs lead to unhealthy emotional outcomes, including depression (for example, *'I will ignore my friend and delete their mobile number, as they clearly don't want to talk to me'*).

The above example illustrates how an activating event – a friend not greeting you in the corridor – can be rationally or irrationally interpreted. Irrational thinking or interpretations lead to unhealthy outcomes, for example, depression; whereas rational and logical thoughts lead to good mental health and happiness.

Evaluation of the Cognitive Approach to Explaining Depression

- One strength of the cognitive explanation for depression is its **application** to therapy. Cognitive explanations have been used to develop effective treatments for depression, including Cognitive Behavioural Therapy (CBT), and Rational Emotive Behaviour Therapy (REBT) which was developed from Ellis's ABC model. These therapies attempt to identify and challenge negative, irrational thoughts and have been successfully used to treat people with depression, providing further support to the cognitive explanation of depression.

- However, one weakness of the cognitive approach is that it does not explain the **origin of irrational thoughts**. Since most of the research in this area is correlational, psychologists are unable to determine if negative, irrational thoughts cause depression, or whether a person's depression leads to a negative mindset. Consequently, it is possible that other factors, for example genes and neurotransmitters, are the cause of depression and the negative, irrational thoughts are the symptom of depression.

- There are **alternative explanations** which suggest that depression is a biological condition, caused by genes and neurotransmitters. Research focused on the role of serotonin has found lower levels in patients with depression. In addition, drug therapies, including SSRIs (Selective Serotonin Reuptake Inhibitors), which increase the level of serotonin, are found to be effective in the treatment of depression, which provide further support for the role of neurotransmitters in the development of depression. This therefore casts doubt on the cognitive explanation as a sole cause of the disorder.

- There is research evidence which supports the cognitive explanation of depression. **Boury et al. (2001)** found that patients with depression were more likely to misinterpret information negatively (cognitive bias) and feel hopeless about their future (cognitive triad). Further to this, **Bates et al. (1999)** gave depressed patients negative automatic though statements to read and found that their symptoms became worse. These findings support different components of Beck's theory and the idea that negative thinking is involved in depression.

Treating Depression

Cognitive treatments for depression are based on the assumption that faulty thinking/thought processes make a person vulnerable to depression. **Cognitive Behavioural Therapy (CBT)** involves both cognitive and behavioural elements. The cognitive element aims to identify irrational and negative thoughts, which lead to depression. The aim is to replace these negative thoughts with more positive and rational ones. The behavioural element of CBT encourages patients to test their beliefs through behavioural experiments and homework.

There are various components to CBT, including:
1) Initial assessment
2) Goal setting
3) Identifying negative/irrational thoughts and challenging these:
    a. Either using Beck's Cognitive Therapy
    Or
    b. Ellis's REBT
4) Homework

There are two different strands of CBT, based on Beck's theory and Ellis's ABC model. All CBT starts with an initial **assessment**, in which the patient and therapist identify the patient's problems. Thereafter, the patient and therapist agree on a set of **goals**, and plan of action to achieve these goals. Both forms of CBT (Beck's and Ellis's) then aim to **identify the negative and irrational thoughts**; however, their approaches differ slightly.

BECK'S COGNITIVE BEHAVIOURAL THERAPY	ELLIS'S RATIONAL EMOTIVE BEHAVIOUR THERAPY (REBT)
If a therapist is using Beck's cognitive therapy, they will help the patient to identify negative thoughts in relation to themselves, their world and their future, using **Beck's negative triad**.	Ellis developed his **ABC model** to include D (**dispute**) and E (**effective**). Like Beck, the main idea is to challenge irrational thoughts; however, with Ellis's theory this is achieved through 'dispute' (argument).
The patient and therapist will then work together to challenge these irrational thoughts, by discussing **evidence for** and **against them**.	The therapist will **dispute** the patient's irrational beliefs, to replace their irrational beliefs with more **effective** beliefs and attitudes.
The patient will be encouraged to test the **validity** of their negative thoughts and may be set **homework**, to challenge and test their negative thoughts.	There are different types of dispute which can be used, including: **logical dispute** – where the therapist questions the logic of a person's thoughts: *'Does the way you think about that situation make any sense?'* Or **empirical dispute** – where the therapist seeks evidence for a person's thoughts: *'Where is the evidence that your beliefs are true?'*

Following a session, the therapist may set their patient **homework**. The idea is that the patient identifies their own irrational beliefs and then proves them wrong. As a result, their beliefs begin to change. For example, someone who is anxious in social situations may be set a homework assignment to meet a friend for a drink.

Evaluation of the Cognitive Approach to Treating Depression

- One strength of cognitive behaviour therapy comes from research evidence which demonstrates its effectiveness in treating depression. Research by **March *et al.* (2007)** found that CBT was as effective as antidepressants in treating depression. The researchers examined 327 adolescents with a diagnosis of depression and looked at the effectiveness of CBT, antidepressants, and treatment with a combination of CBT and antidepressants. After 36 weeks, 81% of the antidepressant group and 81% of the CBT group had significantly improved, demonstrating the effectiveness of CBT in treating depression. However, 86% of the CBT with antidepressant group had significantly improved. This suggests that a combination of both treatments may be more effective.

- One issue with CBT is that it **requires motivation**. Patients with severe depression may not engage with CBT or even attend the sessions and therefore this treatment will be ineffective in treating these patients. Alternative treatments, such as antidepressants, do not require the same level of motivation and may be more effective in these cases. This poses a problem for CBT, as CBT usually cannot be used as the sole treatment for severely depressed patients, who often lack the motivation to attend therapy and to speak about their depression.

- Cognitive behavioural therapy has been criticised for its **overemphasis on the role of cognitions** as the primary cause of depression. Some psychologists have criticised CBT for not taking into account other factors such as social circumstances which might contribute to a person's depression. For example, a patient who is suffering from domestic violence or abuse does not need to change their negative/irrational beliefs, but in fact needs to change their circumstances. Therefore, CBT would be ineffective in treating these patients until their circumstances have changed.

- The success of CBT may not be due to either of the specific techniques advocate by Beck or Ellis. **Rosenzweig (1936)** argued that it is the relationship between the client and the therapist which is of utmost importance in determining the success of a psychological therapy. Simply having someone to talk to may be the crucial component in having a positive outcome rather than the specific techniques adopted by the psychologist. This viewpoint becomes evident when comparison studies such as that conducted by **Luborsky *et al.* (2002)** show very little difference between different methods of psychotherapy.

Extension Evaluation: Issues and Debates

- The cognitive approach for depression considers both **nature and nurture,** since maladaptive thinking, according to Beck, is automatic (nature) but can be modified by experience such as undertaking CBT (nurture). **Soft determinism** is therefore advocated where behaviour is regulated by mediational processes and an individual can dispute their irrational thoughts, with practice.

- The cognitive approach can be considered fairly **scientific** due to the methods used for investigation; however, researchers are unable to directly observe the thinking processes involved for a depressed patient.

Possible Exam Questions

1. Which of the following statements does not fit with Beck's negative triad explanation of depression? (1 mark)
    a. "I have been fired from my job unfairly"
    b. "I was no good at my job anyway"
    c. "I bet there's so many other people who would do the job better than me"
    d. "I'm never going to find another job again"

2. Four possible evaluative statements about cognitive behavioural therapy are listed below. Identify which one of the statements is correct. Only shade **one** box. (1 mark)
    "Cognitive behavioural therapy…"
    a. does not require the therapist to be trained
    b. must only be used in group settings
    c. allows the patient some control over the treatment
    d. has lots of side effects

3. Define what is meant by an irrational thought. (2 marks)
4. Suggest **one** limitation of the cognitive approach to explaining depression. (2 marks)
5. Identify and explain **one** strength of the cognitive approach to treating depression. (3 marks)
6. Describe Beck's negative triad as an explanation for depression. (4 marks)
7. Outline what is involved in cognitive behavioural therapy for treating depression. (4 marks)

8. Rob has recently lost his job of over ten years and his doctor has subsequently diagnosed him with depression. He has been referred to see a cognitive psychologist to better understand his condition. Describe **two** different explanations the cognitive psychologist might use to help Rob understand why he is suffering with depression. (4 marks)

Exam Hint: To gain full credit here students must make clear reference to two different explanations named on the specification, Beck's negative triad and Ellis's ABC model, and how they can be applied to Rob's specific situation now he is unemployed and suffering with depression. For example, losing his job could have been the activating event (A), his irrational belief (B) could be that he will never secure future employment so the consequence (C) is the unhealthy emotional outcome of depression.

9. Describe **one or more** strategy that might be used within a session with a cognitive behavioural therapist or suggested for a patient to try in the treatment of their depression. (4 marks)

Exam Hint: Students need to avoid the trap of wasting time and effort outlining cognitive theory in response to this question. The focus needs to be on describing one or more strategy, such as homework tasks or logical disputing, with the expansion of how this is helpful in the treatment of depression.

10. Discuss the cognitive approach to explaining psychopathology. (8 marks)

Exam Hint: Typically, in shorter essays such as this, the AO2 element of student responses does not usually demonstrate such thorough knowledge and understanding as the description. Students can gain credit for using cognitive behavioural therapy as a means to evaluate the approach.

11. Outline and evaluate the cognitive approach to explaining depression. (12/16 marks)
12. Discuss the cognitive approach to treating depression. (12/16 marks)

Exam Hint: For student responses to appear thorough and well-informed, reference to both Beck's and Ellis's treatments provide breadth and depth, though is not essential. Answers produced must have explicit links to depression, however, and evaluation must not be generic to any approach.

OBSESSIVE COMPULSIVE DISORDER

Specification: The biological approach to explaining and treating OCD: genetic and neural explanations; drug therapy.

WHAT YOU NEED TO KNOW
<ul><li>Outline and evaluate the biological approach to explaining OCD, including:<ul><li>Genetic explanations</li><li>Neural explanations<ul><li>Neurotransmitters</li><li>Brain structure</li></ul></li></ul></li><li>Outline and evaluate the biological treatment of OCD: drug therapy.</li></ul>

Introduction
The biological approach to explaining obsessive compulsive disorder (OCD) addresses both genetic and neural explanations. Genetic explanations suggest that OCD is inherited and that individuals receive specific **genes** from their parents which influence the onset of OCD. Neural explanations suggest that abnormal levels of **neurotransmitters** (e.g. **serotonin** and **dopamine**) and certain regions of the brain are implicated in OCD.

Genetic Explanations
Genetic explanations have focused on identifying specific **candidate genes** which are implicated in OCD. It is believed that OCD is a **polygenic** condition, which means that several genes are involved. **Taylor (2003)** suggests that as many as 230 genes may be involved in the condition and perhaps different genetic variations contribute to the

different types of OCD, e.g. hoarding or obsession with religion. Two examples of genes that have been linked to OCD are the **COMT gene** and **SERT gene**.

The COMT gene is associated with the production of *catechol-O-methyltransferase* (COMT for short), which regulates the neurotransmitter **dopamine**. Although all genes come in different forms, one variation of the COMT gene results in higher levels of dopamine and this variation is more common in patients with OCD, compared to people without OCD.

Secondly, the SERT gene (also known as the 5-HTT gene) is linked to **serotonin** and affects the transport of this neurotransmitter (hence **SER**otonin **T**ransporter). Transportation issues cause lower levels of serotonin to be active within the brain and are associated with OCD (and depression). **Ozaki *et al.* (2003)** published results from a study of two unrelated families who both had mutations of the SERT gene. It coincided with six out of seven of the family members having OCD.

Neural Explanations – Neurotransmitters

The neurotransmitter **serotonin** is believed to play a role in OCD. Serotonin regulates mood and lower levels of serotonin are associated with mood disorders, such as depression. Some cases of OCD are also associated with the reduced levels of serotonin, which may be caused by the SERT gene. Evidence for the role of serotonin in OCD comes from research examining antidepressants (SSRIs) such as that conducted by **Piggott *et al.* (1990)** who found that drugs which increase the level of serotonin in the synaptic gap are effective in treating patients with OCD.

In addition, the neurotransmitter **dopamine** has also been implicated in OCD. In contrast to serotonin, *higher* levels of dopamine have been associated with some of the symptoms of OCD, in particular, the compulsive behaviours.

Neural Explanations – Brain Structure

It is believed that several regions in the frontal lobes of the brain have abnormal brain circuits in patients with OCD. Two brain regions implicated specifically in OCD are: the **basal ganglia** and **orbitofrontal cortex**.

The **basal ganglia** is a cluster of neurons at the base of the forebrain, which is involved in multiple processes, including the coordination of movement. Patients who suffer head injuries in this region often develop OCD-like symptoms.

The **orbitofrontal cortex** is a region which converts sensory information into thoughts and actions. PET scans have found higher activity in the orbitofrontal cortex in patients with OCD when, for example, a patient is asked to hold a dirty item with a potential germ hazard. One suggestion is that the heightened activity in the orbitofrontal cortex increases the conversion of sensory information to actions (behaviours) which results in compulsions.

Evaluation of the Biological Approach to Explaining OCD

- A strength of the biological explanation of OCD comes from research support seen in **family studies**. **Lewis (1936)** examined patients with OCD and found that 37% of the patients with OCD had parents with the disorder and 21% had siblings who suffered. **Nestadt *et al.* (2000)** take this point further and proposes that individuals who have a first-degree relative with OCD are up to *five* times more likely to develop the disorder over their lifetime compared to members of the general population without this genetic link. Research from family studies like this provides support for a genetic explanation for OCD, although it does not rule out other (environmental) factors playing a role.

- Further support for the biological explanation of OCD comes from **twin studies** which have provided strong evidence for a genetic link. **Billett *et al.* (1998)** conducted a meta-analysis of 14 twin studies investigating the genetic inheritance rate of OCD. It was concluded that monozygotic (MZ) twins had *double* the risk of developing OCD compared to dizygotic twins (DZ) if one of the pair had the disorder. Since concordance rates in twin studies are never 100%, it suggests that the **diathesis-stress model** may be a better explanation whereby a genetic vulnerability is inherited and triggered by a stressor in the environment.

- There is an issue with understanding neural mechanisms involved in OCD. While there is evidence which suggests that certain neural systems do not function normally in patients suffering from OCD, such as the basal ganglia and orbitofrontal cortex, research has also identified other areas of the brain that are *occasionally* involved as well. This means that there is no brain system which has consistently been found to play a role in OCD. So, although there is evidence that neurotransmitters and brain structures are implicated, it must not be concluded that there is a **cause and effect relationship** since it is difficult to ascertain whether the biological abnormalities seen are a cause of OCD or the result of the disorder.

- There are credible **alternative explanations** for the development of OCD. For example, the two-process model proposed by behaviourists suggests that learning could play a crucial role in the disorder. Initial learning of the feared stimulus could occur through classical conditioning's associative process where, for example, dirt is paired with anxiety. This behaviour pattern would be maintained through operant conditioning and negative reinforcement whereby the stimulus is avoided so the anxiety is removed. This could result in an obsession forming which is linked to the development of a compulsion, e.g. washing of hands, which serves to reduce the anxiety felt. Support for this alternative explanation is found in the success of behavioural treatments for OCD where symptoms of patients are improved for 60-90% of adults (**Albucher *et al.,* 1998**).

Treating OCD

Biological treatments for OCD aim to restore chemical imbalances in the brain since this is assumed to be the main cause of the disorder. Two types of **drug therapy** are commonly used in the treatment of OCD:
1) Antidepressant drugs
2) Anti-anxiety drugs

Drug Therapies

The biological explanation suggests that OCD is the result of low levels of **serotonin** in the brain. According to **Choy and Schneier (2008)**, **SSRIs** (selective serotonin reuptake inhibitors), a type of **antidepressant** with brand names including *Prozac*, are the preferred treatment option for OCD. Antidepressants improve mood and reduce the anxiety experienced by patients with OCD.

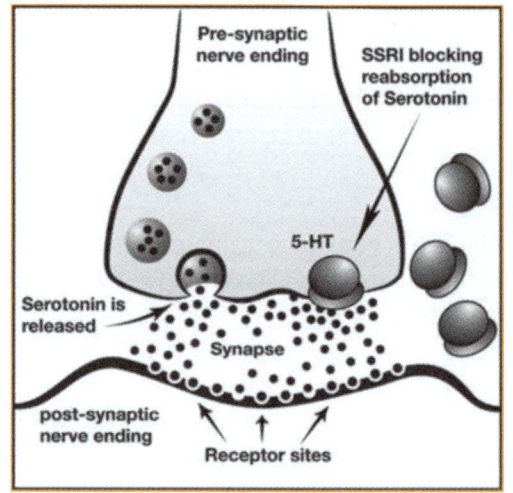

When serotonin is released from the **pre-synaptic cell** into the **synapse**, it travels to the **receptor sites** on the **post-synaptic neuron**. Serotonin which is *not* absorbed into the post-synaptic neuron is **reabsorbed** into the sending cell. SSRIs increase the level of serotonin available in the synapse by *preventing* it from being reabsorbed into the sending cell. This increases the level of serotonin in the synapse which, in turn, improves the concentration of the brain chemical at the receptor sites on the post-synaptic neuron, intensifying the stimulation on the receiving nerve.

Anti-Anxiety Drugs

Benzodiazepines (BZs) are a range of anti-anxiety drugs that include trade names like *Valium* and *Diazepam*. BZs work by enhancing the action of the neurotransmitter **GABA** (gamma-aminobutyric acid). GABA tells neurons in the brain to 'slow down' and 'stop firing' and around 40% of the neurons in the brain respond to GABA. This means that BZs have a general quietening influence on the brain and consequently reduce anxiety, which is experienced as a result of the obsessive thoughts common in OCD.

Some neurons have GABA receptor sites at the synapse and when GABA locks into one of these, the flow of *chloride ions* into the neuron is increased. The *chloride ions* make it more difficult for the receiving neuron to be stimulated by further neurotransmitters. Thus the nervous system is slowed down making the patient feel more relaxed.

Exam Hint: This part of the specification contains a lot of long and complex vocabulary which can confuse some students. Use abbreviations such as SSRIs and BZs to make it easier to remember.

Evaluation of Biological Treatments of OCD

- One strength of biological treatments for OCD comes from research support for their effectiveness. Randomised drug trials compare the effectiveness of SSRIs and a drug with no pharmacological value, called a **placebo**.

Soomro et al. (2008) conducted a review of research examining the effectiveness of SSRIs and found that they were significantly more effective than placebos in the treatment of OCD, across 17 different trials. This supports the use of biological treatments, especially SSRIs, for OCD. However, studies such as this are criticised for only concluding the short-term effectiveness of drug treatments with long-term effects still to be investigated empirically.

- An advantage to biological treatments for OCD is their cost effectiveness. Drug therapies, such as SSRIs and BZs, are relatively **cost-effective** in comparison with psychological treatments, like cognitive behavioural therapy (CBT). Consequently, many doctors prefer the use of drugs to psychological treatments, as they are a more cost-effective solution for treating OCD, which is beneficial for health service providers. In addition, psychological treatments like CBT require a patient to be **motivated** to engage whereas drugs are non-disruptive to everyday life, and can simply be taken until the symptoms subside. As a result, this means that drug treatments are likely to be more successful for patients who lack the motivation to complete intense psychological treatments.

- A limitation of prescribing drug treatments for OCD is the possible **side effects** of drugs like SSRIs and BZs. Although evidence suggests that SSRIs are effective in treating OCD, some patients experience mild side effects like indigestion, while other might experience more serious side effects like hallucinations, erection problems and raised blood pressure. BZs are renowned for being highly addictive and can also cause increased aggression and long-term memory impairments. As a result, BZs are recommended for short-term treatment only of up to four weeks, according to **Ashton (1997)**. Consequently, side effects diminish the effectiveness of drug treatments, as patients will often stop taking medication if they experience negative side effects.

- Drug treatments are criticised for treating the **symptoms** of the disorder and **not the cause**. Although SSRIs work by increasing the levels of serotonin in the brain, which reduces anxiety and alleviates the symptoms of OCD, it does not treat the underlying cause of OCD. Furthermore, once a patient stops taking the drug, they are prone to relapse. **Koran et al. (2007)** suggest that psychological treatments such as CBT may be a more effective long-term solution to provide a lasting treatment and a potential cure.

Extension Evaluation: Issues and Debates

- This explanation for OCD reduces a complex human behaviour to a single gene or brain chemical and so is considered **biologically reductionist**. For example, the biological explanation does not consider the role cognitions (thinking) or learning in the development or maintenance of OCD.

- The biological explanation follows a **nomothetic** approach which suggests the same treatment for all people suffering from OCD, without considering individual differences.

Possible Exam Questions

1. Name the therapy advocated by the biological approach in the treatment of obsessive compulsive disorder (OCD). (1 mark)

2. Suggest **one** limitation of the genetic explanation for obsessive compulsive disorder (OCD). (2 marks)

3. Explain **one** criticism of the neural explanation for obsessive compulsive disorder (OCD). (3 marks)

4. Briefly outline the biological approach to explaining obsessive compulsive disorder (OCD). You may refer to genetic and/or neural explanations in your answer. (4 marks)

Exam Hint: A common error for students to make in a question like this is to muddle up the description of catechol-o-methyl transferase (COMT) and serotonin transporter (SERT) genes and whether serotonin or dopamine might be increased or decreased. Remember that COMT is linked to higher levels of dopamine and SERT to lower levels of serotonin.

5. When investigating psychopathology, researchers often analyse the behaviour of twins. A recent study has revealed that the concordance rate for monozygotic twins (MZ) for obsessive compulsive disorder (OCD) ranges from 45% to 65%. With reference to these statistics, what do the findings seem to suggest about the origins of OCD? (4 marks)

Exam Hint: If a question contains a scenario then be sure to relate your answer directly and repeatedly to the context to achieve maximum credit for your response.

6.   Gwyndaf went to see his doctor who asked him to describe his daily life.

Gwyndaf said: "Sometimes I have thoughts that my family members are in peril. I really worry about them being held at knifepoint by a burglar. I can only calm myself down if I check that all of the doors are locked and windows are shut. A few months ago, this was enough to make me feel at ease but now I have to open and close the doors and check the handles every time to make sure they are really locked. It takes me a long time to get ready to go upstairs to bed at night making sure the house is secure."

Outline **two** characteristics of obsessive compulsive disorder, referring to Gwyndaf in your response. (4 marks)

7.   Evaluate genetic and/or neural explanations of obsessive compulsive disorder (OCD). (6 marks)

8.   Two friends were discussing their peer, Molly, who has recently been diagnosed by her doctor as suffering from obsessive compulsive disorder (OCD).

Stuart says, "It isn't a shock to me that Molly has been diagnosed OCD because her dad is always checking light switches are off and the doors are locked".

Andrew says, "Really? I didn't know that! I always assumed that anyone suffering with OCD had something not working properly in their brains which made them behave differently".

Discuss neural **and** genetic explanations for obsessive compulsive disorder (OCD). Refer to the conversation between Stuart and Andrew in your answer. (12 marks)
Exam Hint: Although this question has a clear context which must be referred to, the command word 'discuss' also requires evaluative commentary. Answers can sometimes be limited if they are only related to perceived general issues with biological explanations rather than those specific to neural and genetic explanations.

9.   Discuss **one or more** biological explanation for obsessive compulsive disorder (OCD). (12/16 marks)
Exam Hint: This question requires both an outline and an evaluation of one (or more) biological explanation for OCD. Successful students must avoid providing overly impressive detail in terms of knowledge at the expenses of a comprehensive discussion/evaluation.

Discuss the biological approach to treating obsessive compulsive disorder (OCD). Refer to research evidence in your answer. (12/16 marks)

PSYCHOPATHOLOGY KEY TERMS

Psychopathology	Psychopathology is the scientific study of mental/psychological disorders. The Psychopathology Topic considers different explanations for various psychological disorders (e.g. depression, phobias and obsessive compulsive disorder), including biological, psychological and social explanations.
Beck's Negative Triad	According to Beck, sufferers of depression experience cognitive distortions. Beck said that people with depression draw irrational conclusions about themselves (nobody loves me), their world (the world is an unfair place) and their future (I will always be a failure). These three distortions form Beck's negative triad.
Behavioural Explanations: Phobias	Behavioural explanations view phobias as a learned behaviour, acquired through classical conditioning and maintained through operant conditioning.
Behavioural Treatments: Phobias	Behavioural treatments are based on the assumption that if a behaviour (e.g. a phobia) is learned , then it can also be unlearned. Behavioural treatments, such as systematic desensitisation and flooding, are based on classical conditioning and the concept of extinction.
Biological Explanations: OCD	Biological explanations for OCD suggest that an individual's genes and/or brain functioning make them vulnerable to developing this disorder.
Biological Treatments: OCD	Biological treatments for OCD are based on the assumption that drugs can be used to rebalance neurochemical imbalances in sufferers. For example, as low levels of serotonin are associated with OCD, SSRIs have been used to try to address this imbalance.
Classical Conditioning: Phobias	The process of classical conditioning can explain how we acquire phobias. For example, we learn to associate something we do not fear, such as a dog (neutral stimulus), with something that triggers a fear response, such as being bitten (unconditioned stimulus). After an association has formed, the dog (now a conditioned stimulus) causes a response of fear (conditioned response) and consequently, we develop a phobia.
Clinical Characteristics: Depression	The clinical characteristics of depression include behavioural, emotional and cognitive symptoms. Behavioural characteristics include loss of energy, disturbances with sleep and changes in appetite. Emotional characteristics include depressed mood, feelings of sadness, and feelings of worthlessness. Cognitive characteristics include a diminished ability to concentrate and difficulties with attention. In addition, cognitive characteristics also include focusing on the negative aspects of the situation, while ignoring the positives and in some cases thoughts of self-harm, death or suicide.
Clinical Characteristics: OCD	The clinical characteristics of OCD include behavioural, emotional and cognitive symptoms. Behavioural characteristics include compulsions (e.g. excessive hand washing). Emotional characteristics include anxiety and distress caused by obsessions, which consist of persistent and/or forbidden thoughts. Cognitive characteristics include obsessive thoughts (obsessions), which are the main cognitive feature of OCD. Sufferers of OCD know that their obsessions and compulsions are irrational, and experience selective attention directed towards the anxiety-generating stimuli.
Clinical Characteristics: Phobias	The clinical characteristics of phobias include behavioural, emotional and cognitive symptoms. Behavioural characteristics of phobias include avoidance. However, if a person is unable to avoid their phobia, this causes panic, which may result in crying, screaming or running away. The key emotional characteristic of phobias is excessive and unreasonable fear and anxiety. Cognitive characteristics include selective attention and irrational beliefs. The person will find it difficult to direct their attention away from the feared object or situation, and their belief about the object or situation is irrational, e.g. all spiders are dangerous/deadly.
Cognitive Behavioural Therapy: Depression	Cognitive Behavioural Therapy is based on both cognitive and behavioural techniques. There are two different strands of CBT, based on Beck's and Ellis's theories. All CBT starts with an initial assessment, in which the patient and therapist identify the patient's problems. Thereafter, the patient and therapist agree on a set of goals, and plan of action to achieve these goals. Both forms of CBT then aim to identify the negative and irrational thoughts; however their approaches are slightly different. Beck's cognitive therapy will help the patient to identify negative thoughts in relation to themselves, their world and their future, using Beck's negative triad. Ellis's Rational-Emotive Behaviour Therapy (REBT) will involve techniques such as empirical argument and logical argument. The patient and therapist will then work together to challenge these irrational thoughts, by discussing evidence for and against them. The patient will be encouraged to test the validity of their negative thoughts and may be set homework, to challenge and test their negative thoughts.

Cognitive Explanations: Depression	Cognitive explanations for depression suggest that faulty thinking/thought processes make a person vulnerable to depression. People with depression often show cognitive distortions, faulty information processing and negative thinking. Cognitive psychologists, such as Beck and Ellis, believe that these thinking patterns are the cause rather than symptoms of depression.
Cognitive Treatments: Depression	Cognitive treatments for depression are based on the assumption that faulty thinking/thought processes make a person vulnerable to depression. Therefore cognitive treatments, such as CBT and REBT, aim to challenge irrational thoughts and replace them with more rational ones.
Definitions of Abnormality	Definitions of abnormality are different methods of defining and diagnosing psychological illnesses. Examples include statistical infrequency, deviation from social norms, failure to function adequately and deviation from ideal mental health.
Deviation from Ideal Mental Health	Deviation from ideal mental health is a definition of abnormality, which suggests that abnormal behaviour should be defined by the absence of particular (ideal) characteristics. Jahoda proposed six principles of ideal mental health, including having a positive view of yourself and being resistant to stress. Therefore, if an individual does not demonstrate Jahoda's criteria, they would be classified as abnormal.
Deviation from Social Norms	Deviation from social norms is a definition of abnormality where a behaviour is seen as abnormal if it violates unwritten rules (social norms) about what is acceptable in a particular society.
Drug Therapies: OCD	Drug therapies are based on the assumption that drugs can cure a neurochemical imbalance, which is seen as the cause of OCD. Two types of drug are used for the treatment of OCD: antidepressants and anti-anxiety drugs. SSRIs (antidepressants) increase the level of serotonin in the synapse and result in more serotonin being received by the receiving cell, thus reducing the symptoms of OCD. Benzodiazepines (BZs) are a range of anti-anxiety drugs, which include trade names like Valium and Diazepam. BZs work by enhancing the action of the neurotransmitter GABA. GABA tells neurons in the brain to 'slow down' and 'stop firing' which means that BZs have a general quietening influence on the brain and consequently reduce anxiety experienced as a result of the obsessive thoughts.
Ellis's ABC Model	Ellis proposed the A-B-C three stage model, to explain how irrational thoughts could lead to depression. The A stands for an activating event (e.g. you pass a friend in the corridor at school, and he/she ignores you, despite the fact you said 'hello'). The B stands for beliefs, which can be either rational or irrational (e.g. an irrational interpretation of the event might be that you think your friend dislikes you and never wants to talk to you again). The C stands for consequences, and according to Ellis, irrational beliefs lead to unhealthy emotional outcomes, including depression (e.g. I will ignore my friend and delete their mobile number, as they clearly don't want to talk to me).
Failure to Function Adequately	Failure to function adequately is a definition of abnormality where a person is considered abnormal if they are unable to cope with the demands of everyday life and live independently in society.
Fear Hierarchy	A fear hierarchy is a process used in systematic desensitization (a behavioural treatment for phobias). The client and therapist work together to develop the hierarchy, where they rank a list of situations relevant to the phobic stimulus from least to most terrifying. After that, the individual is taught relaxation techniques and is then exposed to each situation in the hierarchy while trying to remain relaxed.
Flooding	Flooding is a behavioural therapy of phobias that is based on the idea of extinction. Rather than exposing a person to their phobic stimulus gradually, a person is exposed to the most frightening situation immediately. For example, a person with a phobia of dogs would be placed in a room with a dog and asked to stroke the dog straight away. With flooding, a person is unable to avoid (negatively reinforce) their phobia and through continuous exposure, anxiety levels decrease (extinguish).
Genetic Explanations: OCD	Genetic explanations for OCD suggest that individuals inherit specific genes that cause OCD. Two genes that have been linked to OCD are the COMT gene and SERT gene. The SERT gene (also known as the 5-HTT gene) affects the transport of serotonin and can cause lower levels of serotonin, which is also associated with OCD. COMT is responsible for clearing dopamine from synapses and low activity of the COMT gene is also associated with OCD. It is also believed that OCD is a polygenic condition, which means that several genes are involved.
Irrational Thoughts	According to Ellis, irrational thoughts are patterns of thinking that are illogical, distort reality and prevent you from reaching your goals. They also lead to unhealthy emotions and self-defeating behaviour. Ellis used the ABC model to explain how irrational thoughts affect our behaviour and emotional state, and devised REBT, where the main technique is to identify and dispute such thinking.

Neural Explanations: OCD	Neural explanations for OCD focus on neurotransmitters and brain structures. The neurotransmitter serotonin is believed to play a role in OCD. Lower levels of serotonin (possibly caused by the SERT gene) are associated with OCD. In terms of brain structures, the basal ganglia is involved in multiple processes, including the coordination of movement. Patients who suffer head injuries in this region often develop OCD-like symptoms, following their recovery.
Operant Conditioning: Phobias	Although classical conditioning can explain why we develop a phobia, it struggles to explain why our phobias do not decay (extinguish) over time. According to operant conditioning, phobias can be negatively reinforced. This is where a behaviour is strengthened, because an unpleasant consequence is removed. For example, if a person with a phobia of dogs sees a dog whilst out walking, they might try to avoid the dog by crossing over the road. This avoidance reduces the person's feelings of anxiety and negatively reinforces their behaviour, making the person more likely to repeat this behaviour (avoidance) in the future.
Relaxation	Relaxation is one of the processes involved in systematic desensitization. The client and therapist work together to develop a fear hierarchy and then the client is taught relaxation techniques, such as breathing techniques. The final component of systematic desensitisation involves exposing the patient to their phobic situation (starting at the bottom of the hierarchy and moving up) while remaining relaxed. The idea is that the relaxation should overtake the fear (reciprocal inhibition).
Statistical Infrequency	Statistical Infrequency is a definition of abnormality. According to this definition, a behaviour is seen as abnormal if it is statistically uncommon, or not seen very often in society.
Systematic Desensitisation	Systematic desensitisation uses reverse counter-conditioning to unlearn the maladaptive response to a situation or object, by eliciting another response (relaxation). There are three critical components to systematic desensitisation: 1) Fear hierarchy; 2) Relaxation training; 3) Reciprocal inhibition.
Two-Process Model	According to the two-process model, phobias are initiated through classical conditioning (learning through association) and maintained through operant conditioning (negative reinforcement).

Outline and evaluate two or more definitions of abnormality. (16 marks)

One definition of abnormality is known as the deviation from social norm definition. A social norm is an unwritten rule about what is acceptable within a particular society. Therefore, according to this definition, a person is seen as abnormal if their thinking or behaviour violates these social norms of what is acceptable. For example, if someone was walking around the streets of London naked, you might think they were abnormal. However, this same behaviour in a remote African tribe would be considered perfectly normal as part of their culture.

The first definition is presented clearly and accurately, using an example to demonstrate understanding.

One issue with this definition of abnormality is that social norms change over time, an issue referred to as hindsight bias. For example, homosexuality was regarded as a mental illness in the UK until 1973, often resulting in institutionalisation, but is now simply considered a variation of normal behaviour. This means that, historically, a reliance upon deviation from social norms as a definition of abnormality may have resulted in violations of human rights where people, by today's standards, were deemed 'abnormal'. It could be argued that diagnoses upon these grounds may have been used as a form of social control over minority groups as a means to exclude those who do not conform.

An interesting discussion point about hindsight bias and how it relates to social norms changing over time.

How far an individual deviates from a particular social norm is mediated by the severity of their 'behaviour' and the context. For example, when someone breaks a social norm once this may not be deviant behaviour, but persistent repetition of such behaviour could be evidence of psychological disturbance. Likewise, someone walking topless on a beach would be considered normal but adopting the same attire for the office would be viewed as abnormal and possibly an indication of an underlying psychological problem. As a consequence, this definition fails to offer a complete explanation in its own right, since different conclusions are reached in different situations and contexts.

The evaluative commentary is enhanced by the discussion of context as a mediating factor in determining whether behaviour deviates from social norms.

According to the Failure to Function Adequately (FFA) definition, a person is considered abnormal if they are unable to cope with the demands of everyday life and live independently in society. Furthermore, to be classified as abnormal, a person's behaviour should cause personal suffering and distress because of their failure to cope. However, they may also cause distress or discomfort to other people who observe their behaviour. For example, someone who is suffering from depression may struggle to get out of bed in the morning or they may find it difficult to communicate with their family and friends. Consequently, they would be considered abnormal as their depression is causing an inability to cope with the demands of everyday life (going to work), whilst their behaviour is also causing distress and discomfort to relatives.

A second definition is presented in equal depth to the first and is explained well.

One weakness of the FFA definition stems from individual differences. For example, one person with Obsessive Compulsive Disorder (OCD) may exhibit excessive rituals that prevent them from functioning adequately, as they constantly miss work; whereas another person may suffer from the same excessive rituals, but find time to complete their rituals and always attend work on time. Therefore, despite the same psychological and behavioural symptoms, each person would be diagnosed differently according to this definition, thus questioning the validity of this definition. This issue exemplifies the problem of taking a nomothetic approach in psychology. Definitions of abnormality typically take a nomothetic approach and try to identify a list of factors, or symptoms, that can be used to diagnose abnormal behaviour. However, some psychologists, in particular Humanistic psychologists, would argue that this approach ignores the essence of being human (e.g. individual differences) and therefore an idiographic approach to defining abnormality might be more appropriate.

An excellent argument centred around individual differences is presented.

The essay developed this point further and demonstrates excellent knowledge of the idiographic and nomothetic approach applied to the definitions of abnormality topic.

[~600 Words]

Examiner Style Comments: *Mark Band 4*

This essay demonstrates clear knowledge and understanding of two definitions of abnormality – deviation from social norms and failure to function adequately. Likewise, statistical infrequency or deviation from ideal mental health would have been creditworthy. The description is excellent and supported with viable examples tied to psychopathology. The evaluative commentary is thorough, effective, interesting and focused on the demands of the question. Furthermore, the inclusion of an appropriate issue and debate further demonstrates excellent psychological knowledge. It is worth noting that this essay is lengthy and there is no requirement for a 16-mark essay to be this length. The essay would still achieve mark band 4 without one of the evaluation paragraphs and therefore it is important that students consider how they could use their time effectively in exam conditions to maximise their overall marks.

Raymond is a college student who has recently started hearing voices. Raymond is worried and frightened when he hears the voices, which are usually threatening in nature. Consequently, these voices are interrupting Raymond's life and he is struggling to complete his homework and concentrate in the classroom, and he is growing increasingly worried that he might not get into university because of his condition. While Raymond hasn't explicitly told anyone, his teachers and parents are becoming increasingly worried because he looks stressed and anxious.

Discuss deviation from ideal mental health and failure to function adequately as two definitions of abnormality. Refer to Raymond in your answer. (16 marks)

According to the Failure to Function Adequately (FFA) definition, a person is considered abnormal if they are unable to cope with the demands of everyday life (e.g. social or work life) and live independently in society. Furthermore, to be classified as abnormal, a person's behaviour should cause personal suffering and distress because of their failure to cope. However, they may also cause distress or discomfort to other people who observe their behaviour. Therefore, according to this definition, Raymond could be considered abnormal because his symptoms are causing an inability to cope with everyday life as he is finding it difficult to 'complete his homework'. Furthermore, Raymond's symptoms are also causing distress or discomforted, as 'his teachers and parents' have noticed his stress and anxiety.

Explanation of the FFA definition is clear and coherent.

Application of this definition to the case of Raymond is explicit, using material from the scenario to support the point being made.

One strength of the FFA definition is that is takes into account the subjective personal experiences of people like Raymond. This definition considers the thoughts and feelings of Raymond and the issues he is facing and does not simply make a judgement based on a pre-defined list of symptoms. This suggests that the FFA definition is a useful tool for assessing psychopathological behaviour as it takes into account the effect of a person's symptoms of their everyday life.

Evaluation of the FFA definition is simple yet effective.

However, one weakness of the FFA definition is the issue of individual differences. For example, one person who hears voices may be unable to function adequately, whereas another person may suffer from the same symptoms, but function perfectly well. Therefore, despite the same psychological and behavioural symptoms, each person would be diagnosed differently according to this definition, thus questioning the validity of this definition.

Evaluative commentary for this definition is balanced with a weakness.

Jahoda (1958) took a different approach to defining abnormality, suggesting that abnormal behaviour should be defined by the absence of particular, ideal characteristics. In other words, behaviours which move away, or deviate, from ideal mental health. Jahoda outlined a series of principles, including: having an accurate view of reality; being able to integrate and resist stress; and being able to master your environment including love, friendships, work and leisure time. Therefore, if an individual does not demonstrate one of these criteria, they would be classified as abnormal according to this definition. It could be argued that Raymond does not have an accurate view of reality as he is hearing voices which are not present. Furthermore, he seems to be unable to resist stress as his parents and teachers have noted that he is anxious, and he is unable to master the environment, in particular his school work, as his symptoms are preventing him from completing his homework. Consequently, Raymond would be seen as abnormal, according to this definition.

The second definition described demonstrates clear knowledge and understanding.

Reference to the scenario is consistent throughout the answer.

One strength of Jahoda's definition is that it takes a positive and holistic view. Firstly, the definition focuses on positive and desirable behaviours, rather than considering just negative and undesirable behaviour. Secondly, the definition considers the whole person, considering a multitude of factors that can affect their health and well-being. Therefore, a strength of the deviation from ideal mental health definition of abnormality is that it is comprehensive, covering a broad range of criteria.

An interesting discussion point to consider.

However, one weakness of the deviation from ideal mental health definition is the unrealistic criteria proposed by Jahoda. There are times when everyone will experience stress and negativity, for example, when grieving following the death of a loved one. However, according to this definition, these people would be classified as abnormal, irrespective of the circumstances which are outside their control. With the high standards set by these criteria, how many need to be absent for diagnosis to occur needs to be questioned.

The essay is concluded with a valid weakness of the deviation from ideal mental health definition.

[~600 Words]

Examiner Style Comments: *Mark Band 4*

This essay demonstrates an exceptionally clear understanding of two definitions of abnormality intertwined with the skill of applying these to a novel scenario. The outline knowledge is accurate and detailed, striking a balance between the two definitions in equal depth. The evaluation commentary is thorough, effective and focused on the demands of the question. The application draws upon suitable material from the scenario to provide an interesting discussion.

Outline and evaluate the behavioural approach to explaining phobias. (16 marks)

The two-process model suggests that phobias are acquired through classical conditioning: learning by association, and are maintained through operant conditioning: negative reinforcement. According to the theory of classical conditioning, humans can learn to fear an object or stimulus, such as a dog, by forming an association between the object and something which triggers a fear response, for example being bitten. In this example, the dog, which was originally a neutral stimulus, becomes associated with being bitten, which is an unconditioned stimulus. This pairing leads to the dog becoming a conditioned stimulus, which when encountered will elicit fear, a condition response.

Specialist terminology is used from the outset and defined succinctly.

A good explanation of classical conditioning is applied correctly to the acquisition of phobias, with the use of an example.

According to operant conditioning, phobias are negatively reinforced where a behaviour is strengthened, because an unpleasant consequence is removed. For example, if a person with a dog phobia sees one whilst out walking, they might avoid it by crossing the road. This reduces the person's anxiety and so negatively reinforces their behaviour, making the person more likely to continue avoiding dogs, thus maintaining their phobia.

The second element of the two-process model is well explained to create a comprehensive description of the behaviourist approach.

The behaviourist explanation of phobias is supported by research evidence. Watson & Raynor (1920) demonstrated the process of classical conditioning in the formation of a phobia in Little Albert, who was conditioned to fear white rats. This supports the idea that classical conditioning is involved in acquiring phobias in humans and that generalisation can occur to other phobic stimuli. However, since this was a case study, it is difficult to generalise the findings to other children or even adults due to the unique nature of the investigation.

Research evidence is used effectively to support the behaviourist account of phobias.

A strength of the behaviourist explanation is its application to therapy. These ideas have been used to develop treatments, including systematic desensitisation and flooding. Systematic desensitisation helps people to unlearn their fears, using the principles of classical conditioning, while flooding prevents people from avoiding their phobias and stops the negative reinforcement from taking place. These therapies have been successfully used to treat people with phobias, supporting the effectiveness of the behaviourist explanation in helping people to overcome their phobias.

The evaluative commentary commences with a strength of this approach linked to the treatment of phobias. Both treatments are identified and well explained.

The behaviourist explanation for phobias ignores the role of cognition: phobias may develop because of irrational thinking, not just learning. For example, sufferers of claustrophobia may think: 'I am going to be trapped in this lift and suffocate', which is an irrational thought that is not taken into consideration. Consequently, the behaviourist explanation for the development of phobias has been criticised for being environmentally reductionist, by reducing human behaviour to a simple stimulus–response association. Many psychologists, for example cognitive psychologists, would disagree with this explanation, as they argue that other cognitive factors (e.g. irrational thinking) also play an important role. Furthermore, the cognitive approach has also led to the development of cognitive behavioural therapy (CBT), which is said to be more successful than behaviourist treatments.

The AO3 element of the essay is balanced by the development of a counter-argument highlighting the limitations of this approach to explaining phobias. The use of environmental reductionism is effective and demonstrates further evaluative commentary.

There is a claim that the behavioural approach may not provide a complete explanation of phobias. For example, Bounton (2007) highlights the fact that evolutionary factors could play a role in phobias, especially if the avoidance of a stimulus (e.g. snakes) could have caused pain or even death to our ancestors. Consequently, evolutionary psychologists suggest that some phobias are not learned but are in fact innate, as they acted as a survival mechanism for our ancestors. This is called biological preparedness (Seligman, 1971) and casts doubt on the two-process model since it suggests that there is more involved than learning and that some phobias (e.g. snakes) are not learned, but are in fact innate.

[~550 Words]

An interesting discussion point about biological preparedness.

Examiner Style Comments: *Mark Band 4*

This essay demonstrates a remarkably clear understanding of the two-process model proposed by behaviourists to explain the development and maintenance of phobias. The outline knowledge is accurate and detailed, striking a balance between classical conditioning and operant conditioning well. The evaluation commentary is thorough, effective and focused on the demands of the question, concluding with reference to suitable issues and debates to provide an interesting discussion.

Outline and evaluate the behavioural approach to treating phobias. (16 marks)

There are two behavioural therapies used to treat phobias: systematic desensitisation and flooding. Systematic desensitisation uses counter-conditioning to help patients 'unlearn' their phobias, by eliciting another response: relaxation instead of fear. A patient works with their therapist to create a fear hierarchy, ranking the phobic situation from least to most anxiety-inducing. The patient is also taught relaxation strategies, such as breathing techniques, to help them remain calm when exposed to their fear. Finally, the patient works through their fear hierarchy, starting at the bottom, while trying to remain relaxed at each stage. Systematic desensitisation works on the assumption that two emotional states cannot exist at the same time, a theory known as reciprocal inhibition, and eventually relaxation will replace the fear.

A concise introduction to this essay.

An accurate and detailed description of systematic desensitisation as a treatment for phobias is presented.

One strength of systematic desensitisation comes from research evidence that demonstrates its effectiveness. McGrath *et al.* (1990) found that 75% of patients with phobias were successfully treated using systematic desensitisation. This was particularly true when using *in vivo* techniques in which the patient came into direct contact with the feared stimulus, rather than simply imagining (*in vitro*). This shows that systematic desensitisation is effective when treating specific phobias, especially when using *in vivo* techniques.

The evaluative commentary begins with a suitable strength being identified and well explained, drawing on research to support the point.

However, systematic desensitisation is not effective in treating all phobias. Patients with phobias which have not developed through a personal experience (classical conditioning), such as a fear of snakes, are not effectively treated using systematic desensitisation. Some psychologists believe that certain phobias have an evolutionary survival benefit and are not the result of learning. This highlights a limitation of systematic desensitisation, which is ineffective in treating evolutionary-based phobias which have an innate basis.

The discussion is balanced with a counter-argument.

Flooding is a behavioural therapy which, rather than exposing a person to their phobic stimulus gradually, exposes the individual to the most anxiety-inducing stimulus immediately. With flooding, a person is unable to avoid (negatively reinforce) their phobia and through continuous exposure, anxiety levels eventually decrease. Since the option of employing avoidant behaviour is removed, extinction will soon happen because anxiety is time limited, and as a result,

A second behavioural therapy is outlined in sufficient detail to strike a good breadth and

the fear will eventually subside.

depth trade-off.

One issue with flooding is that it can be highly traumatic for patients since it purposefully elicits a high level of anxiety. Wolpe (1969) recalled a case with a patient becoming so intensely anxious that she required hospitalisation. Although flooding is not unethical as patients provide fully informed consent, many patients do not complete their treatment because the experience is too stressful. Therefore, flooding is sometimes a waste of time and money as not all patients engage in the treatment, which will result in the unsuccessful treatment of their phobias.

An interesting evaluation point is argued here about the ethics of flooding.

An issue for behavioural therapies such as flooding and systematic desensitisation is symptom substitution. This means that although one phobia may be successfully removed through counter-conditioning, another may appear in its place. If symptoms are treated and removed, the underlying cause may remain and simply resurface under a new guise. Research in this area is mixed; however, such criticisms are heavily disputed by behaviourists who claim that behavioural treatments provide an ideal treatment for phobias.

The final evaluation paragraph applies to both behavioural treatments, drawing the essay to a neat conclusion.

[~500 Words]

Examiner Style Comments: *Mark Band 4*

This is a well-structured and coherent essay which provides an accurate and well-detailed account of the two behavioural therapies for treating phobias that are named on the specification: systematic desensitisation and flooding. A range of effective evaluation points to both support and critique these therapies are elaborated well, supported by relevant research studies. The essay is focused and specialist terminology is used effectively throughout.

Jack and Jill are discussing their eight-year-old daughter, Jemimah, who is refusing to go swimming for her friend's ninth birthday party.

Jack says: 'Jemimah has a real fear of the water which she gets from you. Maybe I should go with her and wait outside the pool until she becomes more relaxed. After that, we could try sitting on the edge of the pool and watching the others. Hopefully, she might be encouraged and go in the swimming pool to join her friends'.

Jill says: 'No way, we don't have time for that; I need to go to the supermarket! Let's just drop her off and throw her in the pool; that will sort her out!'

Outline and evaluate two behavioural treatments for phobias. Refer to Jack and Jill's conversation in your answer. (16 marks)

There are two behavioural therapies used to treat phobias: systematic desensitisation and flooding. Systematic desensitisation uses counter-conditioning to help patients 'unlearn' their phobias, by eliciting another response: relaxation instead of fear. Here, Jemimah would work with her therapist to create a fear hierarchy, ranking her phobia of water from the least to most anxiety-inducing situations. For example, her least feared situation might be looking at a picture of a swimming pool and her most feared might be falling into the deep end of a swimming pool. Jemimah would also be taught relaxation strategies, such as breathing techniques, to help her remain calm when exposed to her fear. Finally, Jemimah would work through her fear hierarchy, starting at the bottom, while trying to remain relaxed at each stage. Systematic desensitisation works on the assumption that two emotional states cannot exist at the same time, a theory known as reciprocal inhibition, and eventually relaxation will replace her fear.

A swift start to the essay setting the scene for the rest of the discussion to follow logically and coherently.

A well-detailed description of what is involved in systematic desensitisation with clear application to Jemimah.

One strength of systematic desensitisation comes from research evidence that demonstrates its effectiveness. McGrath *et al.* (1990) found that 75% of patients with phobias were successfully treated using systematic desensitisation. This was particularly true when using *in vivo* techniques in which the patient came into direct contact with the feared stimulus, rather than simply imagining (*in vitro*). This shows that systematic desensitisation is effective when treating specific phobias, especially when using *in vivo* techniques and therefore could be an ideal treatment for Jemimah.

Evaluative commentary effectively elaborated with research support from McGrath et al.

Jack, Jemimah's father, is suggesting an *in vivo* form of systematic desensitisation, as he is putting forward a gradual, step-by-step approach to treat his daughter. For example, the father has created a fear hierarchy starting with sitting in the car at the pool, until the girl calms down, followed by sitting in the viewing area, etc. Jack has also acknowledged that it is important for his daughter to remain relaxed at each stage as she will only progress onto the next stage if she calms down. Based on research evidence (McGrath *et al.*) this is likely to be an effective treatment for Jemimah to help her overcome her phobia of water.

Excellent application of knowledge and understanding to the context.

Flooding is a behavioural therapy which, rather than exposing a person to their phobic stimulus gradually, exposes the individual to the most anxiety-inducing stimulus immediately (e.g. throwing her in the swimming pool). With flooding, Jemimah will be unable to avoid (negatively reinforce) her phobia and through continuous exposure to water, her anxiety levels will eventually decrease. Since the option of employing avoidant behaviour is removed, extinction will soon happen because anxiety is time limited, and as a result, her fear of water will eventually subside.

The second treatment for phobias – flooding – is outlined in sufficient detail to create a good breadth/depth trade-off with systematic desensitisation.

One issue with flooding is that it can be highly traumatic for patients since it purposefully elicits a high level of anxiety. Wolpe (1969) recalled a case with a patient becoming so intensely anxious that she required hospitalisation. Although it is not unethical as patients provide fully informed consent, many do not complete their treatment because the experience is too stressful. Therefore, initiating flooding is sometimes a waste of time and money if patients do not engage in the treatment, which will ultimately fail to treat patients in such cases.

An interesting limitation of flooding is effectively elaborated with reference to the psychologist who devised the treatment.

The mother is suggesting the use of flooding for her daughter as she wants to expose Jemimah to her phobia by placing her in an anxiety-inducing situation to cure her fear. However, while flooding is not seen as unethical when patients provide informed consent, it would not be deemed as appropriate for an eight-year-old, who is unable to provide fully informed consent for herself.

The essay is concluded with excellent application skills demonstrating real engagement with the scenario.

[~575 Words]

Examiner Style Comments: *Mark Band 4*

This is a well-detailed and accurate account of two behavioural treatments for phobias, applied seamlessly to the scenario with Jemimah and her fear of swimming. The use of specialist terminology is excellent and adds clarity and focus to the essay. The evaluation is well-elaborated, thorough and effective, drawing on a range of points to support or show limitations of the treatment in question.

Outline and evaluate the cognitive approach to explaining depression.

(16 marks)

Cognitive theories for explaining depression include Beck's Cognitive Triad and Ellis's ABC Model. Beck claimed depression is caused by negative self-schemas and cognitive biases that maintain a cognitive (negative) triad: a negative view of ourselves, the future and the world around us. According to Beck, depressed people possess negative self-schemas, caused by negative experiences in childhood, for example, criticism from parents. Furthermore, Beck found that depressed people are more likely to focus on the negative aspects of a situation, while ignoring the positives. This distorts information, a process known as cognitive bias, and includes overgeneralising. For example, *'I've failed one test so I will fail ALL of my exams!'*

A clear statement to set the scene for the rest of the essay.

A concise, yet accurate, overview of Beck's Cognitive Triad explanation for depression.

Ellis proposed the ABC three stage model, to explain how irrational thoughts can lead to depression. An activating event (A) occurs, for example, you pass a friend in the corridor at school and they ignore you, when you say 'hello'. Your belief (B) is your interpretation, which could either be rational or irrational. According to Ellis, an irrational belief (e.g. 'my friend must hate me') can lead to unhealthy emotional consequences (C), including depression.

The second explanation of depression is slightly shorter in length, but achieves the breadth/depth trade-off when attempting to describe two cognitive explanations of depression.

One strength of the cognitive explanation for depression is its application to therapy. Cognitive explanations have been used to develop effective treatments for depression, including Cognitive Behavioural Therapy (CBT) and Rational Emotive Behaviour Therapy (REBT), which was developed from Ellis's ABC model. These therapies attempt to identify and challenge negative, irrational thoughts and have been successfully used to treat people with depression, providing further support to the cognitive explanation of depression.

A simple yet effective evaluation point highlights the real-world application of the cognitive approach to treating depression.

However, one weakness of the cognitive approach is that it does not explain the origins of irrational thoughts. Since most of the research in this area is correlational, psychologists are unable to determine if negative, irrational thoughts cause depression, or whether a person's depression leads to a negative mindset. Consequently, it is possible that other factors, for example genes and neurotransmitters, are the cause of depression and the negative, irrational thoughts are the symptom of depression.

An interesting discussion point outlining a major issue in the support for cognitive explanations of depression.

In addition, there are alternative explanations which suggest that depression is a biological condition, caused by genes and neurotransmitters. Research focused on the role of serotonin has found lower levels in patients with depression. In addition, drug therapies, including SSRIs (Selective Serotonin Reuptake Inhibitors) which increase the level of serotonin, are found to be effective in the treatment of depression, which provide further support for the role of neurotransmitters in the development of depression. This therefore casts doubt on the cognitive explanation as a sole cause of the disorder.

The previous evaluation point is further developed with the discussion of alternate explanations.

There is research evidence which supports the cognitive explanation of depression. Boury *et al.* (2001) found that patients with depression were more likely to misinterpret information negatively (cognitive bias) and feel hopeless about their future (cognitive triad). Further to this, Bates *et al.* (1999) gave depressed patients negative automatic thought statements to read and found that their symptoms became worse. These findings support different components of Beck's theory and the idea that negative thinking is involved in depression.

A final effective evaluation point drawing on research support.

[~500 Words]

Examiner Style Comments: *Mark Band 4*

This is a well-detailed an accurate account of the cognitive approach to explaining depression and its contribution to psychology and society. The evaluation is well-detailed, thorough and effective, drawing on a range of strengths and limitations. The use of key terminology is excellent and adds clarity and focus to the essay.

Outline and evaluate the cognitive approach to treating depression. (16 marks)

Cognitive Behavioural Therapy (CBT) involves both cognitive and behavioural elements and typically starts with an initial assessment, in which the patient and therapist identify the patient's problems. Thereafter, the patient and therapist agree on a set of goals, and a plan of action to achieve these goals. While there are different forms of CBT (e.g. based on Beck's and Ellis's theories) the aim to identify the negative and irrational thoughts remains the same, despite the fact their approaches differ. Ellis developed his ABC model to include D (dispute) and E (effective). The idea here is that the therapist will dispute the patient's irrational beliefs, to replace their irrational beliefs with more effective beliefs and attitudes. There are different types of dispute which can be used, including: empirical dispute – where the therapist seeks evidence for a person's thoughts: *'Where is the evidence that your beliefs are true?'* Following a session, the therapist may set their patient homework. The idea is that the patient identifies their own irrational beliefs and then proves them wrong. As a result, their beliefs begin to change.

The process involved for a patient undergoing CBT is described effectively, with reference to Ellis's ABC-DE theory.

One strength of cognitive behaviour therapy comes from research evidence which demonstrates its effectiveness in treating depression. Research by March *et al.* (2007) found that CBT was as effective as antidepressants in treating depression. The researchers examined 327 adolescents with a diagnosis of depression and looked at the effectiveness of CBT, antidepressants, and treatment with a combination of CBT and antidepressants. After 36 weeks, 81% of the antidepressant group and 81% of the CBT group had significantly improved, demonstrating the effectiveness of CBT in treating depression. However, 86% of the CBT with antidepressant group had significantly improved. This suggests that a combination of both treatments may be more effective. While March *et al.* provide some support for cognitive treatments of depression, their research demonstrates that a combination of cognitive and biological treatments is more effective. This suggests that cognitive treatments and explanations do not provide a complete explanation of depression and other factors (namely biological ones) should also be considered.

A very well-elaborated evaluation point with supporting research is discussed in an effective and highly academic manner.

One issue with CBT is that it requires motivation. Patients with severe depression may not engage with CBT, or even attend the sessions and therefore this treatment will be ineffective in treating these patients. Alternative treatments, such as antidepressants, do not require the same level of motivation and may be more effective in these cases. This poses a problem for CBT, as CBT cannot always be used as the sole treatment for severely depressed patients, who often lack the motivation to attend therapy and to speak about their depression.

An interesting critique of CBT as a treatment for depression.

CBT has been criticised for its overemphasis on the role of cognitions as the primary cause of depression. Some psychologists have criticised CBT for not considering other factors such as social circumstances which might contribute to a person's depression. For example, a patient who is suffering from domestic violence or abuse does not need to change their negative/irrational beliefs, but in fact needs to change their circumstances. Therefore, CBT would be ineffective in treating these patients until their circumstances have changed.

The evaluative commentary is concluded with a simple, yet effective, argument about the questionable role of other factors in explaining depression.

[~450 Words]

Examiner Style Comments: *Mark Band 4*

This is a succinct yet sufficiently detailed essay which explains the components of cognitive behavioural therapy (CBT) accurately. The evaluation is generally effective with the first evaluation point embedding a successful reference to a relevant debate in psychology which is pertinent to the demands of the question. The use of specialist terminology related to CBT is consistent throughout the response. A good attempt.

Discuss the biological approach to explaining OCD. (16 marks)

The biological approach to explaining obsessive compulsive disorder (OCD) considers genetic and neural explanations. Genetic explanations suggest that OCD is inherited. Neural explanations for OCD suggest that abnormal levels of neurotransmitters are implicated. OCD is a polygenic condition, which means that several genes are implicated. Taylor (2003) suggests that as many as 230 genes may be involved and different genetic variations contribute to the different types of OCD, e.g. hoarding or obsessions with religion. A gene that has been linked to OCD is the COMT gene which produces *catechol-O-methyltransferase.* This variation regulates dopamine and is more common in patients with OCD, compared to people without OCD.

A breakdown of what the biological approach to OCD entails provides a platform for the rest of the essay.

Specialist terminology is used from the outset and is explained well.

Lower levels of serotonin are also associated OCD. Evidence for this comes from research examining antidepressants (SSRIs). Piggott *et al.* (1990) found that drugs which increase the level of serotonin in the synaptic gap are effective in treating patients with OCD, suggesting that serotonin is a contributory factor.

Effective use of research evidence is used to support the description.

A strength of the biological explanation of OCD comes from research support seen in family studies. Lewis (1936) examined patients with OCD and found that 37% of the patients with OCD had parents with the disorder and 21% had siblings who suffered. Nestadt *et al.* (2000) take this point further and proposes that individuals who have a first-degree relative with OCD are up to five times more likely to develop the disorder in their lifetime compared to members of the general population without this genetic link. Research from family studies like this provides support for a genetic explanation for OCD, although it does not rule out other (environmental) factors playing a role. This explanation for OCD reduces a complex human behaviour to a single gene or brain chemical and so is considered biologically reductionist. For example, the biological explanation does not consider the role cognitions (thinking) or learning in the development or maintenance of OCD and is therefore criticised by behavioural and cognitive psychologists for its overly simplistic view.

The evaluative commentary is well-elaborated, drawing upon family studies in this field of psychology.

Reference to the key issue of reductionism is effortlessly integrated into the response.

Further support for the biological explanation of OCD comes from twin studies which provide strong evidence for a genetic link. Billett *et al.* (1998) conducted a meta-analysis of 14 twin studies investigating the genetic inheritance rate of OCD. It was concluded that monozygotic (MZ) twins had *double* the risk of developing OCD compared to dizygotic twins (DZ) if one of the pair had the disorder. Since concordance rates in twin studies are never 100%, it suggests that the diathesis-stress model may be a better explanation whereby a genetic vulnerability is inherited and triggered by a stressor in the environment.

Another sound evaluation point which extends the discussion.

There are credible alternative explanations for the development of OCD. For example, the two-process model proposed by behaviourists suggests that learning could play a crucial role in the disorder. Initial learning of the anxiety-inducing stimulus could occur through classical conditioning, for example if dirt/germs are paired with anxiety (e.g. becoming ill). Compulsive behaviour (e.g. continual hand washing) is then maintained through operant conditioning and negative reinforcement, as the compulsive behaviour reduces the anxiety associated with the anxiety-inducing stimulus which serves to reinforce the condition. Support for this alternative explanation is found in the success of behavioural treatments for OCD where symptoms of patients are improved for 60–90% of adults (Albucher *et al.,* 1998).

An interesting alternative explanation from the behaviourist approach is offered to conclude the evaluative commentary.

[~550 Words]

Examiner Style Comments: *Mark Band 4*

This is a highly detailed and accurate essay examining the biological explanations of obsessive compulsive disorder (OCD), including reference to genetic and neural explanations. The use of specialist terminology is impressive throughout the response. The evaluation is focused, thorough and effective, drawing upon relevant research studies to support the arguments made. Overall, a remarkable account of the biological explanations for OCD.

Outline and evaluate the biological approach to treating OCD. (16 marks)

Biological treatments work on the assumption that OCD is cause by neurochemical imbalances in the brain, and therefore work to readdress these imbalances. Antidepressant drugs and anti-anxiety drugs are commonly used in the treatment of OCD.

A good introduction linking the treatment rationale to the biological approach.

Selective serotonin reuptake inhibitors (SSRIs) are the preferred biological treatment for OCD. SSRIs increase the level of serotonin available in the synapse by preventing it from being reabsorbed into the sending cell. This increases the level of serotonin in the synapse which, in turn, improves the concentration of the brain chemical at the receptor sites on the post-synaptic neuron, intensifying the stimulation on the receiving nerve. Consequently, SSRIs work to improve mood and reduce the anxiety experienced by patients with OCD.

Excellent use of specialist terminology with reference to antidepressants.

Well-detailed and accurate outline of the mode of action for SSRIs.

Benzodiazepines (BZs) work by enhancing the action of the neurotransmitter GABA (gamma-aminobutyric acid). GABA tells neurons in the brain to 'slow down' and 'stop firing'. Some neurons have GABA receptor sites at the synapse and when GABA locks onto one of these, the flow of chloride ions into the neuron is increased. The chloride ions make it more difficult for the receiving neuron to be stimulated further, thus slowing down the nervous system. This means that BZs produce a relaxing effect and consequently reduce anxiety, which is experienced as a result of the obsessive thoughts common in OCD.

An accurate and detailed outline of BZs is also provided.

One strength of biological treatments for OCD comes from research support for their effectiveness. Randomised drug trials compare the effectiveness of SSRIs with a placebo. Soomro *et al.* (2008) conducted a review of research examining the effectiveness of SSRIs and found that they were significantly more effective than placebos in the treatment of OCD, across 17 different trials. This supports the use of biological treatments, especially SSRIs, for OCD. However, studies such as this are criticised for only concluding the short-term effectiveness of drug treatments with long-term effects still to be investigated empirically. The biological explanation follows a nomothetic approach which suggests the same treatment for all people suffering from OCD, without considering individual differences. Some psychologists suggest that other treatments are better at providing long-term relief for sufferers of OCD and therefore cognitive therapies should be used instead of biological ones.

Research is used well to support the strength of biological treatments being discussed here.

A reference to issues and debates is integrated into the AO3 content.

An advantage to biological treatments for OCD is their cost effectiveness. Drug therapies, such as SSRIs and BZs, are relatively cost effective in comparison with psychological treatments, like CBT. Consequently, many doctors prefer the use of drugs to psychological treatments, as they are a more cost effective solution for treating OCD, which is beneficial for health service providers. In addition, psychological treatments like CBT require a patient to be motivated to engage whereas drugs are non-disruptive to everyday life, and can simply be taken until the symptoms subside. As a result, this means that drug treatments are likely to be more successful for patients who lack motivation to complete intense psychological treatments.

The evaluative commentary is further enhanced with another well-elaborated strength of drug treatments.

A limitation of prescribing drug treatments for OCD is the possible side effects of drugs. Although evidence suggests that SSRIs are effective in treating OCD, some patients experience mild side effects like indigestion, while other might experience more serious side effects like hallucinations, erection problems and raised blood pressure. BZs are renowned for being highly addictive and can also cause increased aggression and long-term memory impairments. As a result, BZs are recommended for short-term treatment only of up to four weeks according to Ashton (1997). Consequently, side effects diminish the effectiveness of drug treatments, as patients will often stop taking medication if they experience negative side effects.

The evaluative commentary is balanced with a limitation of drug effects in reference to the negative side effects which can result from the treatment.

[~575 Words]

Examiner Style Comments: *Mark Band 4*

This response demonstrates sound knowledge and understanding of drug therapies which are advocated by the biological approach to treating obsessive compulsive disorder (OCD). The description is excellent, with an appropriate balance achieved between the outline of SSRIs and BZs. The evaluative commentary is interesting, thorough and effectively elaborated with suitable critiques offered.

Two teachers were talking about their student, Benedict, who has recently been diagnosed with OCD.

Cordelia said: 'I wasn't surprised really. I met Benedict's mother Delilah at parents evening and she told me that Benedict's father, Archibald, has OCD.'

'Oh my', said Alasdair. 'I had no idea. I thought OCD was a neural condition.'

Discuss neural and genetic explanations for OCD and refer to Cordelia and Alasdair's conversation in your answer. (16 marks)

Genetic explanations for OCD suggest that it is inherited because individuals receive specific genes from their parents which influence the onset of the disorder. OCD is a polygenic condition, which means that several genes are involved. Taylor (2003) suggests that as many as 230 genes may be involved and different genetic variations contribute to the different types of OCD, e.g. hoarding or obsession with religion. A gene that has been linked to OCD is the COMT gene which produces *catechol-O-methyltransferase.* This variation regulates dopamine and is more common in patients with OCD, compared to people without OCD. This is what Cordelia is alluding to when she says that Benedict's father, Archibald, also has the condition in that he may have passed it down to his son at birth, giving him the predisposition to develop the condition later in life.

The genetic explanation for OCD is well explained, drawing upon relevant research to support the description.

Effective reference to the scenario drawing on appropriate material.

Neural explanations for OCD suggest that abnormal levels of neurotransmitters are implicated. Lower levels of serotonin are associated OCD. Evidence for this comes from research examining antidepressants (SSRIs). Piggott *et al.* (1990) found that drugs which increase the level of serotonin in the synaptic gap are effective in treating patients with OCD. This explanation is what Alasdair considers to be the cause of the disorder, as he believed that OCD was a neural condition.

The second element of the question is addressed well, although in less detail to remain within the number of marks allocated for AO1.

Application to the scenario is good.

A strength of the biological explanation of OCD comes from research support seen in family studies. Lewis (1936) examined patients with OCD and found that 37% of the patients with OCD had parents with the disorder and 21% had siblings who suffered. This research also support Cordelia's view and suggests that her claim that Archibald has OCD as a result of inheriting the condition from his father is support by psychological research.

The evaluative commentary is well-elaborated and makes excellent use of research studies for support.

While research from family studies provides support for a genetic explanation for OCD, it does not rule out other (environmental) factors playing a role. This explanation for OCD reduces a complex human behaviour to a single gene or brain chemical and so is considered biologically reductionist. For example, the biological explanation does not consider the role cognitions (thinking) or learning in the development of OCD. While Cordelia and Archibald both outline biological explanations, they both fail to acknowledge the possibility of other explanations that could also explain Benedict's behaviour. For example, the two-process model proposed by behaviourists suggests that learning could play a crucial role in the disorder. Initial learning of the anxiety-inducing stimulus could occur through classical conditioning, for example if dirt/germs are paired with anxiety (e.g. becoming ill). Compulsive behaviour (e.g. continual hand washing) is then maintained through operant conditioning and negative reinforcement, as the compulsive behaviour reduces the anxiety associated with the anxiety-inducing stimulus which serves to reinforce the condition.

An interesting alternative explanation from the behaviourist approach is offered with some application to the scenario.

Further support for the biological explanation of OCD comes from twin studies which have provided strong evidence for a genetic link. Billett *et al.* (1998) conducted a meta-analysis of 14 twin studies investigating the genetic inheritance rate of OCD. It was concluded that monozygotic (MZ) twins had *double* the risk of developing OCD compared to dizygotic twins (DZ) if one of the pair had the disorder. Since concordance rates in twin studies are never 100%, it suggests that the diathesis-stress model may be a better explanation whereby a genetic vulnerability is inherited and triggered by a stressor in the environment.

The evaluation is continued with interesting discussion about the genetic link to the disorder coming to a thought-provoking conclusion.

[~550 Words]

Examiner Style Comments: *Mark Band 4*

This is a good response to this application question relating to the case of Benedict and his father, Archibald. The answer provides detailed knowledge of the biological approach to explaining obsessive compulsive disorder (OCD) including both genetic and neural explanations, as demanded by the question, which are highly accurate and detailed. The use of specialist terminology is consistent throughout the response and explained well. Furthermore, the discussion is centred on two strengths of these explanations and provides an in-depth commentary that is thorough and effective.

Revision Checklist

Specification	Content	
DEFINITIONS OF ABNORMALITY	Definitions of abnormality, including deviation from social norms, failure to function adequately, statistical infrequency and deviation from ideal mental health.	☐
CLINICAL CHARACTERISTICS	Behavioural, emotional and cognitive characteristics of phobias, depression and obsessive compulsive disorder (OCD).	☐
PHOBIAS	Behavioural approach to explaining and treating phobias: the two-process model, including classical and operant conditioning; systematic desensitisation, including relaxation and use of hierarchy; flooding.	☐
DEPRESSION	The cognitive approach to explaining and treating depression: Beck's negative triad and Ellis's ABC model; cognitive behaviour therapy (CBT), including challenging irrational thoughts.	☐
OBSESSIVE COMPULSIVE DISORDER	The biological approach to explaining and treating OCD: genetic and neural explanations; drug therapy.	☐

AQA A LEVEL PSYCHOLOGY

EXAM BUSTER

PSYCHOPATHOLOGY

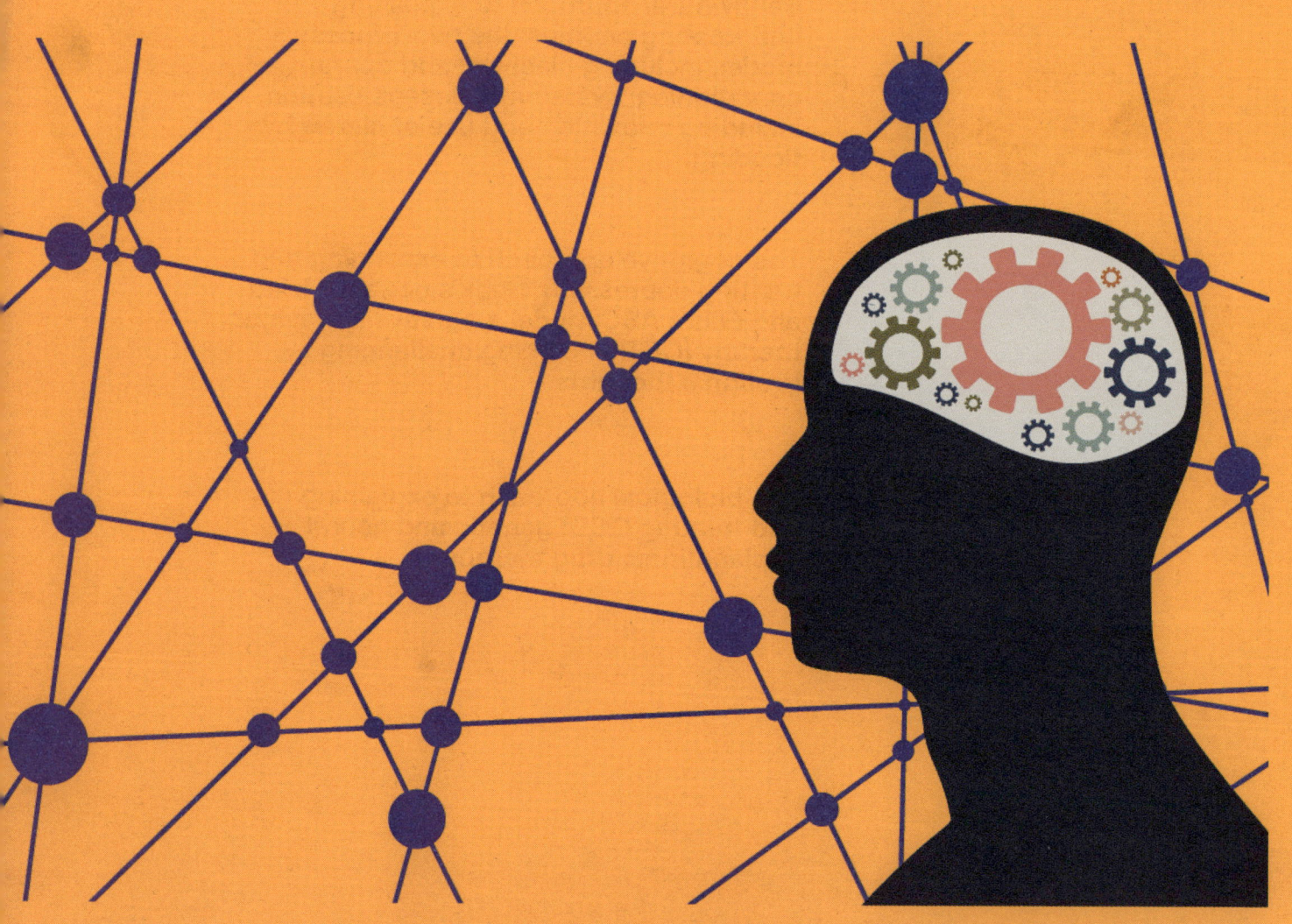

JOSEPH SPARKS & HELEN LAKIN